101 THE BEST WARM SOUPS, EASY TO IMITATE, AND WITH A GERMAN TOUCH!

Delicious soups for starters and main courses.

The German Kitchen

RECIPES TO FALL IN LOVE WITH

Many more cookbooks and recipes on
many other topics, such as
German cuisine, spices, appetizers, and
soups offer you **The German Kitchen**

Published by Mindful Publishing

Mindful Publishing on Instagram:
@mindful_publishing
The German Kitchen on Instagram:
@german.recipes

TABLE OF CONTENT

Red lentils - coconut soup

Curry pumpkin soup

Beef soup

Cheese and leek soup with minced meat

Italian Minestrone

Gyro soup

Spicy duck soup

Chestnut soup

Chopped Vegetable Soup

Wild garlic cream soup

Chickpea soup

Cream of vegetable soup

Strong beef soup

Potato - vegetables - cheese soup

Broccoli cream soup

Celery foam soup

Garlic soup

Swedish summer soup

Strengthening chicken soup

Cream of asparagus soup

Potato soup

Glass noodle soup

Wedding Soup

Tomato soup

Chicken soup

Solyanka

Beetroot soup

Beef soup

Chicken soup with coconut milk

Pumpkin cream soup

Pumpkin soup

Sweet potato soup

Red lentil coconut soup

Asian shrimp soup

Pizza soup

Carrot soup

Pumpkin - coconut - soup

Red lentil curry with coconut milk

Pumpkin soup with red lentils

Cream of mushroom soup

alphabet soup

Cabbage soup

Pumpkin cream soup

Gyro soup

Pea soup

Parsnip cream soup

Goulash soup

Lentil soup

Peas - curry - soup

Fish soup

Green spelt soup

Borscht

Coconut soup

Crab soup

coconut - ginger - carrot soup

Curry sausage soup

Pumpkin coconut soup with red lentils

Kohlrabi - potato - soup

Paprika soup

Cucumber soup

Brussels sprout soup

Ajvar soup

Oxtail soup

Bean stew

Zucchini soup

Fish soup

Tomato soup with feta

Vegetable soup

Chestnut soup

Oatmeal soup

Asparagus soup

Cabanossi - cheese - soup

Mushroom soup

Potato and green asparagus soup

Sweet Potato and Peanut Soup

Rosemary soup

Onion soup

Clear tomato soup with dumplings

bread soup

Cucumber soup

Zucchini soup with cheese

Pumpkin soup

Chestnut cream soup

Red onion soup

Lentil stew

Green spelt soup

GOULASH SOUP

Working time approx. 1 hour
Cooking time approx. 4 hours
Total time approx. 5 hours

Ingredients
1 ½ kg beef goulash meat
800 g potato
400 g onion
2 carrots
3 peppers, red, yellow, green
50 g paprika powder, sweet as a nut
1 teaspoon paprika powder, rose hot
8 tablespoons tomato paste
500 g tomatoes, chunky
1 clove of garlic, pressed
2 tablespoons of sugar
150 g clarified butter
2 tablespoons parsley
2 teaspoons marjoram
2 strips lemon peel, untreated
8 grains allspice
2 bay leaves

1 teaspoon caraway

10 peppercorns, colored or only black

2 cloves of garlic

Chilli pod

200 ml red wine

3 liters chicken broth, warm

2 tablespoons tarragon vinegar

2 tablespoons balsamic vinegar, darker

2 tablespoons white wine vinegar

salt and pepper

Preparation

Cut the onions and fry them in plenty of clarified butter. Stir the onions constantly and fry them gently at low heat for about half an hour until they are nicely browned. Now add 1 pressed clove of garlic, the sugar and the tomato paste, and fry for about 2-3 minutes. Add the paprika powder and fry for another minute. Stir constantly. Then deglaze with the three kinds of vinegar and then with the red wine each time and then bring to the boil briefly. Put the chunky tomatoes and about half of the chicken stock into the kettle and simmer for another 30 minutes.

Put marjoram, allspice seeds, bay leaves, lemon peel, peppercorns, caraway, and garlic into a spice bag, close with kitchen string, and put into the kettle. It is best to fix it with the kitchen string on a pot handle. Put the parsley, and the beef goulash cut into approx. 1 cm pieces into the kettle and let it simmer for at least 2.5 - 3 hours.

Stir regularly and add the remaining stock little by little, depending on taste and consistency.

During this time, cut carrots, potatoes, and peppers into small pieces. Add the carrots 1 h before the end of the cooking time. Potatoes and peppers about 0.5 h before the end. Finally and if necessary, season with salt and pepper and remove the spice bag from the goulash soup. If you like it a little hotter, you can add chilies to the spice bag at the beginning of cooking. Please make sure to keep the long cooking time. This gives the goulash its beautiful brown-red and dark color.

We prepare this goulash soup in a kettle on a gas grill. Of course it can also be prepared over a campfire or in a pot on the stove.

CHICKEN CURRY LEEK SOUP

Menu type: Main course
Servings: 8

Working time approx. 30 minutes
Cooking time approx. 45 minutes
Total time approx. 1 hour 15 minutes

Ingredients
1 kg of chicken breast
2 sticks of leek
600 g mushrooms
2 red bell peppers
2 medium-sized onion
1 cup of cream cheese, approx. 200 g
1 cup of herb processed cheese, approx. 200 g
1-liter poultry stock
150 ml whipped cream
50 ml teriyaki sauce
2 teaspoon curry paste, red
3 tablespoons, heaped flour
2 tablespoons, heaped curry powder
3 tablespoons, heaped parsley, dried

50 g margarine or butter
salt and pepper
oil for frying

Preparation

Clean the leek, cut off the root end, and 2/3 of the green. Cut the rest into rings about 5 mm wide, rinse well and cook in slightly salted water.

In the meantime, wash the chicken breast fillets, cut them into approx. 2 cm pieces and fry them in portions in a large pan in a little oil and set aside.

Wash the peppers, remove the seeds, and cut them into approx. 1 cm pieces. Peel the onions and sauté them together with the paprika in a little oil. After about 5 minutes, add the cleaned and sliced mushrooms and sauté for another 5 minutes, then put aside.

Put the fried chicken pieces back into the pan with the margarine or butter and heat briefly. Add the flour and curry powder, sweat briefly, and then deglaze with the stock. Add the spreadable cheese and let it melt at medium heat while stirring, stir in the cream. Add the prepared paprika-onion-mushroom mixture as well as the cooked leek and season to taste with the Teriyaki sauce, curry paste, and some pepper. With the lid closed, let it stand for about 5 minutes at low heat, stirring occasionally. Finally, stir in the parsley and serve the soup hot.

CHICKEN - NOODLE SOUP

Menu type: Starter
Servings: 4

Working time approx. 20 minutes

Ingredients
125 g Chinese egg noodles
1 tablespoon of oil
4 chicken legs, without skin and bones
1 bunch spring onion, sliced
2 cloves of garlic, chopped
2 cm ginger, fresh, finely chopped
850 ml of chicken broth
200 ml of coconut milk
3 teaspoon curry paste, red
3 tablespoons peanut butter
2 tablespoons soy sauce
1 small pepper, red, diced
60 g peas, frozen
salt and pepper

Preparation
Soften the pasta in a bowl of boiling

water (for about 3-4 minutes).
Heat the oil in a pot or large wok. Add the diced chicken and fry for 5 minutes until it is lightly browned. Add the white pieces of spring onions, garlic and ginger, stir well and cook for 2 minutes. Add the broth, coconut milk, curry paste, peanut butter, and soy sauce, season with salt and pepper, and bring to the boil. Stir and simmer for 8 minutes. Stir from time to time. Add the peppers, peas and the green pieces of spring onions and simmer for another 2 minutes. Add the drained noodles to the soup and heat. Serve the soup in warmed bowls. If you don't like it that hot, just use green curry paste.

PUMPKIN- CARROT- COCONUT- GINGER SOUP

Menu type: Main course
Servings: 2

Working time approx. 15 minutes
Cooking time approx. 20 minutes
Total time approx. 35 minutes

Ingredients
1 onion
¼ Pumpkin, (butternut pumpkin) average size
4 carrot
1 potato
1 tablespoon vegetable broth, instant
2 cm ginger
1 can of coconut milk
1 tablespoon curry paste, (Thai curry paste) red

Preparation

First, dice the onion and sauté until translucent, then add the finely chopped carrots, pumpkin, and potato and also fry briefly. Cut the ginger into small pieces and add them as well. Season quickly with salt and pepper, then add so much water that the vegetables are covered and add the tablespoon Vegetable stock and the Thai curry paste. Calmly rather at the beginning a little less, because you can always add some more if you like it hotter. Add coconut milk as well and let it simmer for about 15 - 20 minutes.

Before you puree the soup, try the vegetables to see if they are cooked nice and soft and if necessary add some Thai curry paste. Then puree everything with the blender and add some more milk or water depending on the desired consistency.

The ginger and Thai curry paste gives the soup a great taste.

VEGAN CURRY-LENTIL SOUP

Menu type: Main course
Servings: 6

Working time approx. 15 minutes
Cooking time approx. 30 minutes
Total time approx. 45 minutes

Ingredients
800 ml vegetable broth
400 ml coconut milk
2 red bell peppers
2 carrot
1 onion
3 teaspoon curry paste, red
180 g lentils, red

preparation
Coarsely chop the vegetables for the soup. Heat
some oil in a pot and fry the vegetables. Lightly
season with salt and pepper. Add the curry paste
and also briefly sauté. Add broth, coconut milk
and the lentils and let everything simmer for
about 25 minutes. Then puree with a blender.

TOMATO SOUP

Menu type: Main course
Servings: 6

Working time approx. 10 minutes
Cooking time approx. 30 minutes
Total time approx. 40 minutes

Ingredients
1,600 g tomato, 2 large cans
400 ml coconut milk
2 large onion
4 cloves of garlic
300 ml vegetable broth
3 tablespoons mango chutney, sweet
Lemon juice
2 tablespoons tomato paste
Marjoram
Oregano
Nutmeg
Rosemary
Thyme
Paprika powder
Pepper

Preparation

Dice and fry the onions and garlic, deglaze with the vegetable stock, add the tomatoes, coconut milk and mango chutney and bring to the boil. Then puree everything and season to taste with the remaining Ingredients.

LENTIL SOUP

Menu type: Main course
Servings: 4

Working time approx. 50 minutes
cooking time approx. 35 minutes
Total time approx. 1 hour 25 minutes

Ingredients
200 g lentils
300 g potato
100 g carrot
100 g celeriac
100 g leek
1-liter vegetable stock
1 tablespoon butter
3 tablespoons balsamic vinegar bianco
parsley, smooth or chives

Preparation
Cut carrot, celery and leek into tiny
cubes. Cut the potatoes into cubes with
an edge length not exceeding 5 mm.
Wash the lentils, drain and simmer with
500 ml vegetable stock for 30 minutes.
In a second pot, melt the butter and briefly

sauté the vegetables with the potatoes. Deglaze with 500 ml vegetable stock and simmer for 5 minutes. Add the lentils and mix everything well. Flavor with vinegar.

Finely chop parsley or chives and garnish the filled plates with them.

POTATO SOUP WITH VEGETABLES

Menu type: Main course
Servings: 4

Working time approx. 20 minutes
Cooking time approx. 30 minutes
Total time approx. 50 minutes

Ingredients
1 large carrot or 2 small
400 g potato
200 g celery
1 bell pepper
150 g spring onion
750 ml water
Salt
1 onion
20 g butter
1 vegetable stock cube, also 2
100 g crème fraîche
Pepper

Cayenne pepper
Nutmeg
Cumin

Preparation
Peel the carrot, 100 g potatoes and the celery. Then cut all three Ingredients and the pepper into small cubes. Cut the green side of the spring onions into fine rings.

Heat the water with a little salt and cook the vegetables until they are firm to bite. Drain the vegetables and collect the cooking water. Finely chop the onion and the white part of the spring onion. Then melt the butter in the pot and sauté the onions until translucent.

Meanwhile peel the remaining potatoes and cut them into pieces. Add to the onions together with the collected cooking water and the vegetable stock. With the lid closed, cook until the potatoes are done.

Add the crème fraîche and the spices. Puree until there are no more pieces. Then season again to your taste.

Finally serve with the cooked vegetable cubes and a few herbs.

GREEN PEA SOUP

Menu type: Main course
Servings: 4

Working time approx. 15 minutes
Cooking time approx. 30 minutes
Total time approx. 45 minutes

Ingredients
1 bag of peas, approx. 450 g
250 g potatoes
1 stick of leek, or spring onions
¾ Litre of broth
salt and pepper
Marjoram
Horseradish
100 g herb cream cheese
Olive oil

Preparation
Briefly fry the peeled potatoes and the leeks in
olive oil. Add half of the peas and pour on the
broth. Cook the soup until done and season
to taste with the spices. Puree, stir in the
cream cheese and add the remaining peas.
Let it simmer.

CHEESE AND LEEK SOUP VEGETARIAN

Menu type: Main course
Servings: 4

Working time approx. 20 minutes
Cooking time approx. 40 minutes
Total time approx. 1 hour

Ingredients
60 g fine soya schnitzel
Water
750 ml vegetable broth
2 ½ Stalks leek
1 pack cream cheese
1 pack herb cheese
50 g cheese (Gouda, Emmental, etc.)
2 cloves of garlic
1 small onion
spice mixture for hunter's mince
or salt, pepper, paprika
Worcester sauce

1 tablespoon of oil
½ teaspoon. mustard

Preparation
Place the soya chips in a saucepan with
a little water and 2 tablespoon hunter's
malt seasoning or salt, pepper, and paprika
and brings to the boil. When the water
has evaporated, add the oil and fry.

Chop the onions, press the garlic and fry briefly.
Add the mustard and a dash of Worcester
sauce. Season again if necessary, the soya
mince should taste slightly overdone.

Cut the leeks into rings and add, deglaze with
the stock and simmer for about 20 minutes
on low heat. Add the cheese and stir until it
has completely melted. Flavour again.

We always offer this soup as a vegetarian
variation on the classic with minced meat.
Therefore I always have the butcher pack some
spice for hunter's meat. If this is not available, you
can also season with salt, pepper, and paprika.

CREAMY POTATO SOUP

Menu type: Main course
Servings: 4

Working time approx. 30 minutes
Total time approx. 30 minutes

Ingredients
750 g potatoes
1 onion
1 stick of leek
1 medium carrot
1-liter vegetable stock
100 ml cream
2 tablespoons of oil
salt and pepper
Nutmeg
Parsley, chopped

Preparation
Cut the onion into small cubes and fry it in
the oil until transparent. Cut the leek into
rings and the carrot into thin sticks and steam
briefly. Pour on the stock, cut the potatoes into

small cubes, and add. Let everything simmer for about 30 minutes. Remove half, puree, and then add again. Stir in the cream and season with salt, pepper and nutmeg. Sprinkle soup with chopped parsley before serving.

CREAMY PUMPKIN SOUP

Menu type: Main course
Servings: 4

Working time approx. 30 minutes
Cooking time approx. 30 minutes
Total time approx. 1 hour

Ingredients
2 kg pumpkin flesh
500 g carrot
1 kg potato
2 Onion
2 tablespoons of butter
2 liters vegetable stock, instant
½ Cup of milk
salt and pepper
possibly pumpkin seeds

Preparation
Cut the pumpkin into slices, peel and remove the seeds. Dice into small pumpkin pieces. Peel and wash carrots, onions, and potatoes and cut them into small pieces. Peel and chop the onions.

Heat the fat and sauté the onion cubes in it. Add stock and bring to the boil. Now add the pumpkin, carrots, and potatoes. Season with salt and pepper. Let it cook for about 20 - 30 minutes while turning the heat down to a low flame. Puree the soup with a blender, add milk and season to taste.

MEDITERRANEAN PUMPKIN SOUP

Menu type: Starter
Servings: 4

Working time approx. 25 minutes
Total time approx. 25 minutes

Ingredients
750 g pumpkin with peel
6 Tomato
1 onion
4 garlic clove
4 sprigs of rosemary, fresh
salt and pepper
4 tablespoons of olive oil
500 ml vegetable broth
75 g olives, black, pitted
Parmesan, coarsely grated

Preparation
Preheat the oven to 220°C.
Halve the pumpkin, remove seeds and cut into pieces. Wash and halve the tomatoes. Peel the onion and cut into rings. Peel the garlic cloves.

Place the vegetables in an ovenproof dish and spread the rosemary sprigs on top. Salt generously and sprinkle with fresh pepper from the mill. Drizzle olive oil over them and roast them in a preheated oven for about 50 minutes. Then let it cool down and remove the rosemary.

Boil up the vegetable stock. Add the vegetables and puree finely with a blender. The result is a creamy, viscous soup.

Chop the olives and add. Re-heat the soup and arrange on plates. Sprinkle with coarsely grated Parmesan and serve.

CARROT - GINGER - HONEY SOUP

Menu type: Starter
Servings: 4

Working time approx. 30 minutes
Total time approx. 30 minutes

Ingredients
1 onion
50 g butter
1 clove garlic
1 tablespoon vegetable oil
2 pieces of ginger
1 stick of celery
500 g carrot, in fine slices
¾ Litres of vegetable stock
1 tablespoon honey
2 tablespoons crème fraîche
salt and pepper
1 lemon, grated zest
Parsley, for decoration

Sugar

Preparation

Chop the onions finely. Peel and slice the ginger and heat the oil and butter. Fry the onion and garlic, add the ginger, celery, and carrot slices and fry with a piece of butter. Deglaze with the vegetable stock, add some salt and simmer for about 12 minutes with the lid closed. Then puree the cooked vegetables with the honey, crème fraîche, a pinch of butter, and grated lemon peel. Season to taste with salt, pepper, lemon juice and sugar and garnish with parsley.

LEEK CREAM SOUP

Menu type: Starter
Servings: 4

Working time approx. 10 minutes

Ingredients
1 stick of leek
1 tablespoon of oil
1 tablespoon of flour
750 ml broth
250 ml cream
1 egg yolk
Parsley

Preparation
Cut the leek into rings, wash and braise
in the fat. Dust the flour over it and
pour the stock over it - let it boil.
Take the pot from the heat, whisk the
cream with the egg yolk and stir in.
Finally sprinkle parsley over it.

RED LENTILS – COCONUT SOUP

Menu type: Main course
Servings: 4

Working time approx. 10 minutes
Total time approx. 10 minutes

Ingredients
2 garlic clove
2 Onion
2 tablespoons of oil
175 g lentils, red
1 tin of tomato (425 ml)
1 can of coconut milk (425 ml)
600 ml vegetable stock, instant
2 teaspoons chili powder
1 teaspoon turmeric
salt and pepper
Coriander, ground

Preparation
Peel and finely dice the garlic and onions. Heat the oil in a pot. Sauté the garlic and onions in it. Add the lentils and fry briefly while turning.

Deglaze with canned tomatoes, coconut milk and stock. Bring everything to the boil and simmer for 20 minutes. Mash the tomatoes with a wooden spoon. Season the soup with chili powder, turmeric, salt, pepper and coriander.

CURRY PUMPKIN SOUP

Menu type: Main course
Servings: 4

Working time approx. 15 minutes
Cooking time approx. 40 minutes
Total time approx. 55 minutes

Ingredients
1 Hokkaido pumpkin
100 ml cream
1 tablespoon sherry
2 tablespoons of butter
1 onion
500 ml vegetable broth
2 tablespoon curry powder
1 pinch of sugar
salt at will
Pepper to taste
Nutmeg at will

Preparation
First remove the seeds from the pumpkin and dice
it. Fry in butter with the diced onion. Deglaze

with the sherry, add the stock and let it cook
for about 20 - 30 minutes. Then add the cream
and the curry powder and puree the soup.
If necessary, let the soup boil down a
little more and then season to taste with
salt, sugar, pepper and nutmeg.

BEEF SOUP

Menu type: Main course
Servings: 6

Working time approx. 40 minutes
Cooking time approx. 1 hour 30 minutes
Total time approx. 2 hours 10 minutes

Ingredients
2 leg slices from beef
500 g of soup meat
3 marrow bones
2 pieces oxtail à 5 - 6 cm
2 Onion
1 stick of leek
125 g celeriac
2 carrot
1 bunch of parsley
2 bay leaves
20 peppercorns
10 allspice grains
½ tablespoon thyme, dried
Salt
2 liters of water

Preparation

Cut the onions in half. Heat a large soup pot without fat. Place the onion halves in the pot with
the cut surfaces facing down and fry until brown.
Then add bones, oxtail, leg slices and soup meat.
Cut the vegetables into small pieces and spread
over them. Fill up with water. Add spices and salt.
Cook for 30 minutes in an open pot, repeatedly
skimming off the foam that forms. The meat
should be covered with water. If necessary, add
some hot water. Then cover the meat and let
it cook lightly at low heat for another hour.
30 minutes before the end of the cooking
time, remove the meat from the broth, pour
the broth through a sieve into another pot
and lightly squeeze the cooked vegetables
with the back of a spoon so that the
vegetable juice gets into the broth.
Serve the soup hot.

CHEESE AND LEEK SOUP WITH MINCED MEAT

Menu type: Main course
Servings: 4

Working time approx. 15 minutes
Cooking time approx. 20 minutes
Total time approx. 35 minutes

Ingredients
500 g minced meat, mixed
3 sticks of leek
250 g processed cheese
1 cup of crème fraîche, approx. 150 g
3 cubes of vegetable stock
700 ml water
2 small baguettes to bake
salt and pepper, from the mill
3 tablespoons of oil
Nutmeg
Garlic powder
Onion powder

Preparation

Preheat the oven to 175 °C top/bottom heat. Place the baguettes in the preheated oven and bake for about 10 minutes.

Meanwhile, put oil in a large pot. Brown the minced meat well on all sides and season with salt and pepper. Cut the leek into small rings and add to the minced meat. Fry for about 5 minutes. Pour in the water, add the stock cubes, and let everything simmer on a low heat for about 10 minutes. Stir in the processed cheese and let it melt. Stir in the crème fraîche and bring to the boil again briefly. Season the soup with salt, pepper, nutmeg, garlic and onion powder to taste.

ITALIAN MINESTRONE

Menu type: Main course
Servings: 8

Working time approx. 30 minutes
Cooking time approx. 1 hour 35 minutes
Total time approx. 2 hours 5 minutes

Ingredients
3 garlic clove
3 large onion
2 sticks of celery
2 large carrot
2 large potatoes
100 g beans, green
100 g courgettes
60 g butter
50 ml of olive oil
60 g bacon, streaky, diced
1 ½ Litre of vegetable broth or chicken broth
100 g tomato, chopped
2 tablespoons tomato paste
1 bunch basil, fresh, finely chopped

100 g parmesan rind
salt and pepper
85 g spaghetti, broken into small pieces
Parmesan

Preparation
Chop the garlic, onions, celery, carrots,
potatoes, beans, and zucchini.

Heat the butter and oil in a large pot and fry
the bacon for 2 minutes. Add garlic and onions,
fry for 2 minutes, then add celery, carrots, and
potatoes and fry for another 2 minutes. Add
the beans to the pot and fry for 2 minutes. Stir
in the zucchini and fry for another 2 minutes.
Put the lid on and steam the vegetables
for 15 minutes, stirring occasionally.

Add stock, tomatoes, tomato paste, basil and
cheese rind and season to taste. Bring to the
boil, reduce the temperature, and simmer
gently for 1 hour. Remove the cheese rind
and throw away. Put the spaghetti pieces
in the pot and cook for 10 minutes.

Serve in large, preheated soup plates sprinkled
with freshly grated Parmesan cheese.

GYRO SOUP

Menu type: Main course
Servings: 4

Working time approx. 20 minutes
Cooking time approx. 20 minutes
Total time approx. 40 minutes

Ingredients
400 g chicken breast fillet
2 tablespoons gyros spice
2 garlic clove
salt and pepper
Curry
some olive oil for frying
4 Onion
4 Bell peppers, colored
1 medium pointed cabbage
1 can of tomato, diced
250 ml cream, cream fines or similar
500 ml vegetable broth (it can be a bit spicy)
200 g processed cheese Preparation Cut
the chicken meat into strips and mix
with the olive oil and gyros spice.

Brown the onions in the oil and add the meat

and fry until it is hot. Now add the pepper strips, the tomatoes, the chopped garlic, and the sliced cabbage. Now fill up with the broth and let it simmer for about 15 - 20 minutes.

Finally, add the cream and the processed cheese and let it simmer until the processed cheese has melted.

Season to taste again with salt and pepper.

SPICY DUCK SOUP

Menu type: Main course
Servings: 4

Working time approx. 30 minutes
Total time approx. 30 minutes

Ingredients
400 g duck breast
3 Chilli pepper, red
3 spring onion
100 g oyster mushrooms
½ bunch basil (Thai basil), alternatively normal basil
3 cloves of garlic
3 tablespoons fish sauce
1 can of coconut milk
500 ml broth (poultry broth)
Oil, for frying
2 tablespoons chili sauce, hot

Preparation
Cut the duck breast into fine strips. Halve chiles
lengthwise, if desired (because of the pungency)

remove seeds and cut into thin strips. Cut spring onions into rings (also the green one). Clean oyster mushrooms (do not wash!!!) and tear or cut into strips. Cut Thai basil (alternatively normal basil) into fine strips. Cut garlic cloves into fine slices. First, sear the meat in a little oil in portions. Remove from the pot and keep warm. Mix the slices of garlic and spring onion with the chili strips, heat up with 3 tablespoons fish sauce in the same pot in which the meat was fried. Add the oyster mushrooms, 2 - 3 tablespoons hot chili sauce, coconut milk (shake vigorously before opening), poultry stock, and the roasted duck meat. Simmer over medium heat for 5 minutes, then add the basil strips (save some for garnishing) and cook for another 1 minute. Serve garnished with basil strips. Although it is a soup, I like to add scented rice as a side dish, so that those who don't want it that hot can soften the heat a bit by eating some rice every now and then. Rice

CHESTNUT SOUP

Menu type: Main course
Servings: 4

Working time approx. 10 minutes
cooking time approx. 35 minutes
Total time approx. 45 minutes

Ingredients
3 small onion, finely chopped
100 g butter
400 g chestnut, cooked, peeled
750 ml vegetable stock
350 ml cream
125 ml of milk
Salt
Sugar
some cinnamon powder

Preparation
Heat the butter and sauté the onions in
it until translucent. Add the chopped
chestnuts and top up with the stock.
Cook on a low heat for 30 minutes.

Then add the cream and milk and simmer
for another 5 minutes. Puree finely with the

blender and season to taste with the spices.

CHOPPED VEGETABLE SOUP

Menu type: Main course
Servings: 4

Working time approx. 30 minutes
Cooking time approx. 1 hour 10 minutes
Total time approx. 1 hour 40 minutes

Ingredients
500 g minced meat, half beef, half pork
500 g potato
500 g carrot
2 large onion
1 tin of kidney beans
1 cup of crème fraîche
1-liter broth
4 tablespoons tomato paste
2 tablespoons marjoram, dried
4 tablespoons of oil
salt and pepper
Sugar

Preparation

Peel potatoes, carrots, and onions and cut into cubes. Fry in oil for about 5 minutes. Add minced meat and tomato paste and fry for another 5 minutes. Add the kidney beans and deglaze with broth so that the vegetables are covered. Add marjoram and a pinch of sugar. Let simmer for about 30 minutes.

Add crème fraîche and cook lightly for another 30 minutes. Season to taste with salt, pepper, and possibly some more sugar.

WILD GARLIC CREAM SOUP

Menu type: Main course
Servings: 6

Working time approx. 20 minutes
Cooking time approx. 10 minutes
Total time approx. 30 minutes

Ingredients
1 small onion
80 g butter
50 g flour
100 ml white wine, dry
750 ml of meat broth
250 g cream
150 g crème fraîche
salt and pepper
Sugar
20 wild garlic leaves
1 egg yolk
some lemon peel, grated, untreated
3 slices of toast

Preparation

Peel and finely dice the onion, then fry in 50 g butter. Add flour and stir until smooth. Pour in white wine, stock, and 150 g cream. Let everything boil for about 3 minutes while stirring. Add crème fraîche and season the soup with salt, pepper, and a pinch of sugar. Wash the wild garlic, dab dry and chop finely. Add to the soup. Then puree the soup with the blender. Remove the crusts from toast, cut into cubes and roast in the remaining butter until golden brown.

Shortly before serving, whisk the egg yolk with the rest of the cream, let it slowly flow into the soup, and whip it with the blender. Add the lemon zest and season to taste. Do not boil any more! Bread

CHICKPEA SOUP

Menu type: Main course
Servings: 4

Working time approx. 20 minutes
Total time approx. 20 minutes

Ingredients
1 tin of chickpeas
1 large sweet potato (batata)
1 paprika sausage (Chorizo, Britzer,
possibly Merguez)
150 g yogurt, white
1 courgette
1 tablespoon paprika pulp
1 tablespoon tomato paste
500 ml beef stock
1 bunch of parsley, smooth
1 onion
2 cloves of garlic
Cumin
Coriander
Turmeric
Harissa
salt and pepper

Preparation

Cut the onion into half rings, dice the batata and fry both in olive oil. Fry the paprika and tomato paste briefly and deglaze with the broth. Add the drained chickpeas and season to taste with the spices (without the parsley) and simmer for 5 minutes. Then add the sausage and the zucchini cut in half and let it simmer for another 5 minutes.

In the meantime, mix the yogurt with the grated garlic and salt, and if you like, you can also add fresh mint. Chop the parsley finely. Arrange the soup and put a good blob of yogurt in the middle, put the parsley around the yogurt. If you like, you can also add a little harissa to the yogurt for the spiciness.

CREAM OF VEGETABLE SOUP

Menu type: Main course
Servings: 4

Working time approx. 20 minutes
Cooking time approx. 30 minutes
Total time approx. 50 minutes

Ingredients
1 pumpkin (Hokkaido)
½ Onion
Oil, for frying, e.g. olive oil
1 vanilla pod
some cumin
some curry powder
1 small chili pepper, dried, not too hot
Nutmeg, freshly grated
1-liter vegetable stock
1 sprig of rosemary, smaller, as required
200 ml cream, or soy cream
salt and pepper

Preparation

Free the Hokkaido from stalk and root, halve in the middle and remove seeds and flesh by hand. Then roughly cut the pumpkin in half. Also, dice the onion roughly. Heat some oil in a pot and add the pumpkin pieces and the diced onion. Sauté the vegetables lightly and let them take some color.

Scrape out the pulp from the vanilla pod and put it in the pot together with the pod. Steam briefly, but do not let it get too hot. Then season with cumin, curry, chopped chili, and nutmeg. Stir well once again and then add the stock. Remove the roast from the bottom of the pot and mix everything well. Let the soup simmer for about half an hour. If you like, add a small sprig of fresh rosemary.

When the cooking time is over, remove the pot from the heat, remove the rosemary and vanilla pod, pour on the cream, and finely puree everything with a blender. Finally, season the soup with salt and pepper.

STRONG BEEF SOUP

Menu type: Main course
Servings: 4

Working time approx. 40 minutes
Cooking time approx. 2 hours
Total time approx. 2 hours 40 minutes

Ingredients
2 Leg slice of beef
2 marrowbone of beef
2 liters of water, cold
½ Tuber Celery
2 carrot
½ Rod Leeks
1 large onion
1 small bunch of parsley
4 juniper berry
Parmesan rind, some pieces if available
some salt and pepper

Preparation
Wash the leg slices and marrow bones under
cold water and soak them in a large bowl of

water for about 30 minutes, then drain.

Meanwhile, clean the vegetables. Cut the celery into cubes about the size of your thumb, carrots, leek, and onion into slices or rings about 1/2 cm thick.

Place the meat and bones in a large pot with about 2 liters of cold water. When the water starts to get hot, grey-brown foam rises, skim it off with a large spoon or a skimmer and discard it.

When the liquid boils effervescently and there is no more foam, the vegetables can be added. Also the juniper berries, 1 tablespoon of salt, and a few turns of the pepper mill. If you do not like to eat the parsley, you can add it in the bunch, then it can be easily removed afterward. Otherwise, simply chop it finely with the stalks and add it.

Cook for about 5 minutes at full heat, then turn down to medium heat and simmer for at least 2 hours without the lid. If you have more time, you can also let it simmer for 3 hours, which makes the meat all the more tender. In any case, the liquid should have reduced by half.

Then take out the leg slices and bones and cut the meat into small cubes. Put the meat and bones back into the pot. Now also add the pieces of parmesan rind. (Before doing so, scrape the top surface of the cheese rind with a knife to remove the protective layer of the Parmesan cheese).

POTATO - VEGETABLES - CHEESE SOUP

Menu type: Main course
Servings: 4

Working time approx. 25 minutes
Total time approx. 25 minutes

Ingredients
500 g potato
1 bunch of carrot
2 sticks of leek
1 head of broccoli
700 g minced meat
1 ½ Pack processed cheese (chives and Gouda or herbs and light cheese)
1 onion
1 ½ Litre of vegetable stock
salt and pepper paprika, garlic, etc.
Paprika powder
Garlic powder
Parsley or chives, finely chopped, for garnishing

Preparation
Peel, wash and cut potatoes into medium-sized pieces, wash, peel and slice carrots. Cut the leek into slices, divide broccoli into florets, chop onions.

Fry the minced meat in a large pan in hot oil and season, add the onions and fry everything very vigorously, then put aside. With lots of paprika, the minced meat gets a nice color when fried.

Place the stock in a sufficiently large pot, add the potatoes and carrots and bring the soup to the boil and simmer for about 10 minutes. Then add leek and broccoli and simmer quietly for another 10 - 15 minutes. Then add the processed cheese, it is best to pluck off small pieces and stir carefully until the cheese has melted. Finally add the fried minced meat to the soup, stir carefully again. Serve sprinkled with parsley or chives!

BROCCOLI CREAM SOUP

Menu type: Main course
Servings: 2
Total time approx. 15 minutes

Ingredients
300 g broccoli
¼ Liters of water
⅛ Liters of cream
¼ liters of chicken stock or soup powder
salt and pepper
3 tablespoons of flour
3 tablespoons of butter
1 spring onion

Preparation
Blanch the broccoli in salted water for 5 minutes,
let it cool down. Heat butter and fry finely
chopped young onion briefly, add flour and cook
to a light roux. Stir in broccoli together with
the cooking water and chicken stock, bring
to the boil briefly and puree with a blender,
add cream, salt and pepper, stir and taste.

CELERY FOAM SOUP

Menu type: Main course
Servings: 4

Total time approx. 20 minutes

Ingredients
400 g celeriac, peeled and finely diced
2 shallot, pulled off and finely diced
1 clove of garlic, peeled and finely diced
2 tablespoons of butter
500 ml vegetable broth, (instant)
100 ml white wine, (dry)
250 g sweet cream
2 slices of toast bread, crushed and debarked
4 tablespoons of olive oil
1 tablespoon oil, (truffle oil)
3 tablespoons butter, (cold), approx. 30 g
2 tablespoons sweet cream, whipped
salt and pepper

Preparation
Heat butter and sauté celery, shallots, and
garlic in it. Deglaze with white wine and

vegetable stock, bring to the boil briefly, add cream and simmer the soup at medium heat in an open pot for about 30 minutes. Then puree the soup, pass through a fine sieve and season to taste with salt and pepper.

Heat the olive oil in a pan and toast the diced toast bread until golden brown. Drain on a kitchen paper and salt lightly.

Bring the soup to the boil again briefly before serving and add the truffle oil. Stir the butter in smaller pieces with the whipped cream into the soup. Cream the soup, spread it on plates, and add croutons.

GARLIC SOUP

Menu type: Main course
Servings: 6

Working time approx. 25 minutes
Total time approx. 25 minutes

Ingredients
1 bulb of garlic, large
150 g onion
40 g butter or margarine
800 ml of meat broth
2 tablespoons vinegar (white wine vinegar)
500 ml whipped cream
80 g Parmesan cheese
2 egg yolks
salt and pepper, white, from the mill
½ Bunch of chives, chopped

Preparation
Place the whole garlic bulb in a preheated oven at 200°C on a medium heat for 30 minutes (fan oven 25 minutes).

Cut the onions into fine cubes and sauté them in a pot with butter or margarine, then add the meat broth and simmer covered on a low heat for about 20 minutes. Meanwhile, peel the cloves of the slightly cooled garlic bulb. Add the garlic to the soup and puree it with the magic wand. Add cream and bring to the boil briefly.

Season the soup with salt, pepper and the white wine vinegar. Whisk the 2 egg yolks in a cup with some soup and beat them with a whisk under the almost boiling soup. Remove the soup from the heat, arrange it and sprinkle with coarsely grated Parmesan cheese and the chopped chives.

SWEDISH SUMMER SOUP

Menu type: Main course
Servings: 4

Working time approx. 20 minutes
Total time approx. 20 minutes

Ingredients
3 large potatoes
1 stick of leek
2 tablespoons of butter
¾ Litres of vegetable stock
200 g salmon fillet
100 ml cream
3 tablespoons dill, chopped

Preparation
Wash, peel and dice the potatoes. Wash the leeks and cut into rings. Fry them both lightly in melted butter. Add the vegetable stock and cook everything for 15 minutes. If necessary, puree them very lightly with the blender (only a few pulses). Cut the salmon into bite-sized cubes and add to the soup. Leave everything

to stand for another 5 minutes. Refine the soup with cream and sprinkle with dill. Serve hot.

STRENGTHENING CHICKEN SOUP

Menu type: Main course
Servings: 4

Working time approx. 30 minutes
Cooking time approx. 3 hours
Total time approx. 3 hours 30 minutes

Ingredients
1 soup chicken or 800 g chicken giblets
1 bunch of carrot
1 celeriac
1 kohlrabi
2 Parsley root
1 bunch of parsley, smooth, fresh
1 ½ Litre of water, as required
Salt
200 g noodles, (vermicelli or other soup noodles)

Preparation
Place the soup chicken, fresh or frozen, in approx. 1 1/2 l salted water. A fresh chicken from the farmer is ideal. Cook for 2 - 3 hours until soft, so that it forms fat on the surface. If

you like, you can also add vegetable broth.

Then clean all the soup vegetables, cut them into small pieces and add them to the stock and cook until al dente.

Take the chicken out and you can add small pieces of meat to the soup. In the end you add the soup noodles, which were cooked in salted water, to the soup. Garnish with fresh parsley.

It is also possible to serve only the broth without meat, noodles, and vegetables to the sick to rebuild their strength. Depending on the patient's appetite, the individual Ingredients can be left in the chicken soup.

It has long been known: when you have a cold it helps to slurp a chicken soup. It is an ancient household remedy and was already known in the Middle Ages. The chicken has a lot of zinc in the breast, which helps well during a flu epidemic. In addition, the hot soup and the vapors stimulate the mucous membranes of the nose so that they can swell. Likewise, the hot steam of the hot soup makes the respiratory tract so hot that viruses cannot hold on.

CREAM OF ASPARAGUS SOUP

Menu type: Main course
Servings: 2

Working time approx. 10 minutes
cooking time approx. 35 minutes
Total time approx. 45 minutes

Ingredients
300 g asparagus, white
1-liter brew, (asparagus brew)
2 tablespoons of butter
3 tablespoons of flour
200 g cream
Pepper, colored, from the mill
Salt
Sugar
nutmeg, grated as freshly as possible
crème fraîche
Chives, cut into small rolls

Preparation

As I often prepare asparagus during the season, I always first boil the asparagus peels and ends in lightly salted water with a little butter and sugar for about 15 minutes, remove and dispose of them with a skimmer, I prepare an ideal basis for my soup. I let this stock cool down, freeze it and use it again next time to cook asparagus. I repeat this until the end of the asparagus season, boiling the fresh peels and ends beforehand each time. Depending on the frequency, the taste of the broth becomes more and more intense. Of course, you have to add some water, salt, sugar and butter if necessary, so that the amount of stock remains constant.
When I prepare the soup, I first cut the peeled asparagus into bite-sized pieces. One last time I boil the peels and ends and then let the asparagus pieces simmer in this old broth for about 10 minutes.

In the meantime, I prepare a roux, which I mix with some asparagus stock and cream, and add to the stock with the asparagus. While stirring, I bring everything to the boil again briefly and vigorously and season with sugar, pepper, salt, and nutmeg. If the soup is still too runny, I bind it again with some flour dissolved in a little water until the consistency suits me. Before serving, I add 1 tablespoon of crème fraîche and 1 tablespoon of chives to each plate.

POTATO SOUP

Menu type: Main course
Servings: 4

Working time approx. 10 minutes
Cooking time approx. 20 minutes
Total time approx. 30 minutes

Ingredients
1 kg potato
4 carrot
1 bunch of soup vegetables
2 tablespoons vegetable stock, instant
3 pairs of Vienna sausages

Preparation
Peel and chop the potatoes and carrots. Chop the soup vegetables also coarsely. Everything does not have to be so precise. Then place everything in a large pot with so much water that the vegetables are just covered and cook in the vegetable stock until done. Then turn everything through a straining mill (Flotte Lotte).

Season again with salt and vegetable stock and, if the soup is too thick, dilute with water. But it may be thick, that's how I like it best. In the end cut the wieners into slices and add them.

GLASS NOODLE SOUP

Menu type: Main course
Servings: 6

Total time approx. 45 minutes

Ingredients
2 liters chicken broth
500 g chicken breasts in strips
1 tablespoon ginger, finely chopped
1 bunch spring onion with green, cut into rings
3 carrot, cut into strips
1 small can of bean sprouts
1 tin of bamboo shoots
½ Pepper, red, cut into strips
2 eggs
2 tablespoons of oil
100 g glass noodles
15 g Mu-Err mushrooms, dried
3 tablespoons cornflour
8 tablespoons soy sauce
4 tablespoons vinegar (rice vinegar)
2 tablespoons tomato paste

1 teaspoon sugar
2 teaspoons Sambal Oelek
4 tablespoons oil (sesame oil), dark

Preparation

Pour boiling water over the dried Mu-Err
mushrooms and let them stand until they
are soft, then cut them into strips.
Pour boiling water over the glass noodles as
well, leave to stand for 5 - 6 minutes, drain
and cut into shorter pieces with scissors.
Chop ginger, cut meat and vegetables into strips
or rings. Drain bean sprouts and bamboo shoots.
Mix the eggs and bake an omelet in oil.
Cut the omelet into fine strips.
Mix the starch with soy sauce, rice vinegar,
tomato paste, sugar, sesame oil, and
sambal oelek until smooth.
Boil up the chicken stock with the chopped
ginger, add the chicken breast strips and simmer
for 5 minutes. Add the Mu-Err mushroom
strips, carrot sticks, and pepper strips as well as
the starch-soy sauce mixture and bring to the
boil briefly. Add the remaining vegetables, the
omelet strips, and the glass noodles, heat up
again briefly, and season to taste if necessary.

WEDDING SOUP

Menu type: Main course
Servings: 6

Total time approx. 45 minutes

Ingredients
500 g minced beef
1 tin of asparagus (cuttings)
1 bunch of soup vegetables
5 medium-sized eggs
some milk, possibly
3 liters of vegetable broth, possibly more or less
1 bunch of parsley
salt and pepper
1 bunch of chives

Preparation
Cut the greens and, if necessary, the asparagus into bite-sized pieces. Season the minced meat with salt, pepper, and a little bit of the chives in a bowl and beat 1 egg over it.

Knead well with wet hands. Then form the mixture into small balls and let everything simmer in the broth on medium heat for about 45 minutes.

For the egg break, whip the remaining
4 eggs in a freezer bag. Season with salt,
pepper and a little bit of the parsley and
mix well with a whisk (if you like, you can
stretch the mixture a bit with milk).

Let the tightly closed bag simmer in a water
bath for about 20 minutes, turning occasionally.
When the mixture is firm, remove the egg
pouch from the freezer bag and cut it into
bite-sized pieces on a cutting board. Add
to the soup 10 minutes before the end of
the cooking time and simmer again.

At the end of the soup again with pepper, salt,
chives and parsley season rice, potatoes

TOMATO SOUP

Menu type: Main course
Servings: 8

Total time approx. 30 minutes

Ingredients
2 kg tomato, ripe
1 celeriac
1 carrot
1 leek stick
2 Onion
100 g tomato paste
2 liters chicken broth
2 garlic clove
1 sprig of rosemary
2 sprigs of thyme
1 sprig of basil
1 sprig of oregano
2 teaspoons sugar
salt and pepper
200 ml cream
1 tablespoon crème fraîche
2 tablespoons of butter
100 g smoked beef
175 g rice

1 tablespoon parsley, finely chopped

Preparation

Clean and coarsely chop the onions, leek, carrot, and celery, finely dice the smoked beef, lightly crush the garlic cloves. Cut the tomatoes into quarters and remove the stalk.

Heat the butter and let the onions, leek, celery, and carrots in it lightly take color. Add the smoked beef and continue to fry until everything begins to brown well. Add the tomato paste, stir, and brown. After about 1 minute, add the tomatoes, heat while stirring and let it stew for about 10 minutes. Then fill up with the chicken stock, add sugar and herbs, bring the soup to a boil and simmer gently for 1 hour.

Cook the rice according to the instructions on the packet.

Pass the tomato soup through a sieve and put it back into the pot. Add the rice, pour on the cream, and bring to the boil again. Refine with crème fraîche and season with salt, pepper, and parsley. Rice

CHICKEN SOUP

Menu type: Main course
Servings: 4

Working time approx. 20 minutes
Cooking time approx. 20 minutes
Total time approx. 40 minutes

Ingredients
500 g chicken breast
2 carrot
1 parsnip
½ Celeriac
1 leeks
200 g peas, frozen
150 g mussel noodles
1-liter chicken broth
some salt and pepper
6 allspice grains
2 bay leaves
1 teaspoon turmeric
½ teaspoon nutmeg
4 stems of oregano, fresh
10 stems of parsley
1 tablespoon olive oil for frying

Preparation

Peel and dice the carrots, parsnip, and celery. Wash, clean, and slice the leeks. Wash the chicken breast, pat dry, and cut into small cubes. Wash the oregano and parsley, spin dry and chop finely.

Heat the olive oil in a large pot. Sauté the carrots, parsnip, celery and leek in it. Pour the chicken stock over the vegetables and bring to the boil. Add the allspice seeds and bay leaves and cook for about 10 minutes.

Put the chicken breast and the mussel noodles in the pot. Season the soup with oregano, curcuma and nutmeg, mix well and let it boil for about 5 minutes.

Add the peas to the soup, season with salt and pepper, and simmer for another 5 minutes. Finally, fish the bay leaves and allspice seeds out of the soup and stir in the chopped parsley.

Arrange the soup on deep plates and garnish with some parsley.

SOLYANKA

Menu type: Main course
Servings: 4

Total time approx. 35 minutes

Ingredients
200 g salami
200 g hunting sausage
200 g poultry sausage
200 g bacon, diced
5 medium-sized onion
4 bell pepper
150 g tomato paste, more depending on taste
5 Gherkin and cucumber water
1 tablespoon of Sambal Oelek or
1 dried chili pepper
1 bay leaf
Broth, fat (best is a stock cube, then it
works great with the dosage)
½ tablespoon mustard
3 cloves of garlic
soured cream

Preparation
Fry the bacon, add the diced sausage, (not yet

the salami!), fry everything nicely. Then add the salami, continue frying briefly, add the onion to the pot and continue frying until the onions are glassy. If it starts to set, add a little water. Now add the diced peppers, the tomato paste and the crushed garlic, fry a little. Then add the chopped cucumbers, some cucumber water, and all the spices. Add 1 to 1 1/2 liters of water, add the fatty stock and simmer for 20 minutes.

BEETROOT SOUP

Menu type: Main course
Servings: 4

Working time approx. 30 minutes
Cooking time approx. 40 minutes
Total time approx. 1 hour 10 minutes

Ingredients
4 tubers beetroot (approx. 1 kg)
300 g bacon, smoked
2 onions, diced
1 ½ Litre of vegetable stock
1 cup of sour cream
1 tablespoon marjoram
Thyme
salt and pepper
Lovage, grated or ground
some lemon juice, possibly
some water, possibly
Boiled potatoes

Preparation
The Red Prayers wash and cook. After
cooking, peel the skin and grate the tubers
coarsely on a kitchen grater.

Cut the pancetta into small cubes and fry it together with the diced onions in a large pan. Deglaze with the vegetable stock and add the grated beetroot. If necessary, add some more water, depending on how thick the soup is now.

Now season to taste with the specified spices. Mix the sour cream in a separate bowl with a small amount of the hot soup, then add it to the soup (this prevents the cream from curdling).

Now possibly season with some lemon juice (approx. 1 teaspoon) - not too much, so that it does not get too sour. The soup is properly seasoned if you don't want to stop tasting it. Boil boiled potatoes spread them on the plates, and pour the soup over them.

BEEF SOUP

Menu type: Main course
Servings: 6

Total time approx. 45 minutes

Ingredients
2 kg of soup meat
some meat and marrow bones
3 carrot
2 sticks of leek
½ Celeriac
1 onion
1 bunch of parsley, bay leaves and thyme branches
1 chili pepper
1 tablespoon of peppercorns
4 grains all spice
1 teaspoon. mustard seeds
1 tablespoon of salt
3 liters of water
some parsley
200 g ribbon noodles

Preparation
First, layout a large soup pot with the bones.
In the case of the marrow bones, make sure

to press out the marrow first. This is easier if the bones have been watered beforehand. The marrow should not be added to the broth, as this would lead to cloudiness. Place the meat on the bone bed.

Clean the vegetables. Cut the onion in half, remove only the outermost skin and fry the onion with the skin on the cut surfaces in a pan without oil until very dark.

Coarsely chop 2 carrots, 1 leek, and the celery and add them to the pot with the herb bouquet, onion and spices and fill up with water. Bring everything slowly to the boil without a lid. Do not skim off the foam that forms, this will clear the soup, provided that the soup never boils effervescent, but simmers quietly. Leave the soup to simmer below the boiling point for about 3 hours. When the meat is soft, take it out and pour the stock through a fine sieve. Discard the cooked vegetables and bones and cut the meat into bite-sized pieces and set aside.

Bring the broth to the boil again, slice 1 carrot and 1 leek, add to the broth with parsley and let it simmer. Cook the ribbon noodles al dente, add to the stock with the meat, and serve immediately.

CHICKEN SOUP WITH COCONUT MILK

Menu type: Main course
Servings: 6

Working time approx. 30 minutes
Cooking time approx. 25 minutes
Total time approx. 55 minutes

Ingredients
2 cans of coconut milk à 400 ml
¼ Litres of chicken broth
5 stems lemongrass
7 cm Galangal, peeled, sliced
3 chilies, whole, red
3 tablespoons fish sauce
8 Kaffir lime leaves (Bai Magrood)
400 g chicken breasts, cut into
small cubes or strips
150 g mushrooms, quartered (or
fresh straw mushrooms)
2 lime, the juice

fish sauce, to taste
1 teaspoon palm sugar, possibly a little
more (or refined sugar)

Preparation

Cut the lemongrass into 4 cm long pieces and
tap them lightly with the back of a knife.
Bring the broth and half of the coconut milk
to the boil and add the lemongrass, galangal,
Magrood leaves and chilies, season with the
fish sauce, and simmer for 10 minutes.

Add the mushrooms and cook for another 5
minutes, then stir in the chicken meat and
cook for a few minutes on low heat, it must
remain tender. Add the remaining coconut
milk and season with lime juice, sugar and
fish sauce. Arrange in bowls and garnish with
chili strips, spring onions, and coriander.
The soup should taste freshly
sour and slightly salty.

PUMPKIN CREAM SOUP

Menu type: Main course
Servings: 8

Total time approx. 20 minutes

Ingredients
2 Hokkaido pumpkins
800 g carrot
2 medium potatoes
¼ Tuber Celery
1 piece of ginger, approx. 7 cm
2 small chili peppers
1 garlic clove
1 medium-sized onion
1.2 liters of vegetable stock
1 can of coconut milk
1 tablespoon curry powder
salt and pepper
Nutmeg
Oil

Preparation
Remove seeds from pumpkin and chilies,

peel carrots, potatoes, ginger, onions, celery and garlic. Cut everything into cubes and fry briefly in a large pot in a little oil. Dust with curry powder and deglaze with the broth. Let it simmer at low heat for about 30 minutes.

When all vegetables are soft, puree the soup with the blender. If it's too creamy, add some more vegetable stock. Season to taste and stir in the coconut milk. Heat again and pass through with the blender jug, then serve.

PUMPKIN SOUP

Menu type: Main course
Servings: 4

Working time approx. 20 minutes
cooking time approx. 35 minutes
Total time approx. 55 minutes

Ingredients
1 Hokkaido pumpkin, approx. 600 g, diced
1 piece ginger, finely chopped
1 onion, finely diced
1 can of unsweetened coconut milk
1 tablespoon curry paste, red
500 ml vegetable broth
1 potato, finely diced
possibly pumpkin seeds
possibly ginger, cut into slices

Preparation Heat the cream of the coconut milk
in a pot. Add the onions, ginger, and curry paste
and sweat for 3 - 4 minutes. Add the pumpkin
cubes and potatoes and steam for 3 minutes.

Deglaze with coconut milk and vegetable stock.
Cook the vegetables for about 30 minutes until
soft, then puree and pass through a sieve.

SWEET POTATO SOUP

Menu type: Main course
Servings: 4

Working time approx. 20 minutes
Cooking time approx. 40 minutes
Total time approx. 1 hour

Ingredients
1 kg carrot
500 g sweet potato
1 ½ Litre of vegetable stock
1 large vegetable onion
1 bunch of parsley, curly
3 tablespoons tomato paste
½ cup of olive oil
2 cups of crème fraîche
1 teaspoon heaped ginger root
1 teaspoon heaped paprika powder, noble sweet
1 tablespoon curry powder
some salt
some pepper, black

Preparation

Cut the unpeeled carrots and the peeled sweet potatoes into small cubes. Finely chop the onion and parsley.

In a large pot, fry the onion cubes in the olive oil until translucent, then add the tomato paste and fry briefly. It must not burn, otherwise, it becomes very bitter. Now put the carrot and sweet potato cubes into the pot and steam for about 4 minutes, then add the vegetable stock and simmer for about 30 minutes at medium heat until the vegetables are nice and soft and easily decompose. Puree everything with a blender until a creamy consistency is reached. Grate the ginger with a fine kitchen grater and add 1 teaspoon. of it to the pot. Add the curry and paprika powder, crème fraîche, and finely chopped parsley, stir well and season to taste with salt and pepper.

RED LENTIL COCONUT SOUP

Menu type: Main course
Servings: 4

Working time approx. 10 minutes
Cooking time approx. 20 minutes
Total time approx. 30 minutes

Ingredients
1 tin of pizza tomatoes (400 g)
1 can of coconut milk (400 g)
1 onion
175 g lentils, red
3 teaspoons chili powder
2 teaspoons turmeric
600 ml vegetable broth
Sunflower oil
Salt

Preparation
Peel the onions and cut them into fine cubes.
Sauté in sunflower oil until translucent. Add
red lentils, tomatoes with juice and coconut
milk and stir well. Add the vegetable stock

and simmer the soup for about 20 minutes.

Finally season with salt, chili,
and turmeric powder.

ASIAN SHRIMP SOUP

Menu type: Main course
Servings: 4

Working time approx. 15 minutes
Cooking time approx. 10 minutes
Total time approx. 25 minutes

Ingredients
250 g shrimp, peeled
2 cloves of garlic
1 piece of ginger (walnut-sized)
1 stick of leek
300 g carrot
½ Bunch of dill
1 tablespoon of oil (soya oil)
2 teaspoons curry paste, red, possibly more
1 chili pepper, possibly
¾ Litres of chicken broth
250 ml of coconut milk
2 tablespoons lemon juice
1 teaspoon sugar
salt and pepper, colorful

Preparation

Wash the peeled shrimps. Peel and finely chop the garlic and ginger. Clean and wash the leek and cut it into rings. Clean, wash and peel the carrots, cut lengthwise into strips, then dice finely. Wash the dill and pat dry.

Heat the soya oil in a pot. Add the prawns, ginger, and garlic and fry over a moderate heat for 1 - 2 minutes. Remove and put aside on a plate.

Add some more soy oil to the same pot if necessary. Add the curry paste, carrots, leek and sugar and stir-fry for 2 - 5 minutes, add chicken stock, and coconut milk. Bring to the boil and simmer gently until the vegetables are cooked.

Season the soup with lemon juice, salt, pepper, and chopped dill. Put the prawns, garlic, and ginger back into the soup and let it steep for about 2 minutes. Flavour again.

Arrange in soup plates and garnish with dill and the chili pepper cut into thin strips.

PIZZA SOUP

Menu type: Main course
Servings: 10

Total time approx. 20 minutes

Ingredients
1 kg minced meat, (from beef)
3 cans of mushrooms
1 pack tomato, happened
6 Pepper, (tricolor)
3 cups of cream
3 cups of crème fraîche
600 g cream processed cheese
salt and pepper
Pizza spice
Broth, instant

Preparation
Fry the minced meat with salt and pepper
until crumbly, then add the mushrooms (with
juice) and the strained tomatoes. Stir and add
the chopped peppers. Let it cook for about 10
minutes. Then add the cream and the crème
fraîche and mix. Finally, add the processed
cheese and season again with the spices. If

necessary add some more instant stock. When the cheese has melted, you can serve the soup. Baguette goes best with it.

CARROT SOUP

Menu type: Main course
Servings: 2

Working time approx. 20 minutes
Cooking time approx. 2 hours
Total time approx. 2 hours 20 minutes

Ingredients
500 g carrot
1 liter of water
Water or broth to refill
3 g salt, preferably Himalaya salt
Meat bones or chicken breast fillet

Preparation
Let the peeled carrots simmer in water
for about 2 hours. Then puree them and
fill up the soup again with boiled water
or broth to 1 liter. Add the salt.

For the taste you can also cook chicken. Before
I put the carrots in the pot, I boil a broth
from meat bones, remove the meat from the
bones later and serve it with the soup.

PUMPKIN - COCONUT - SOUP

Menu type: Main course Portions: 4

Working time approx. 30 minutes
Total time approx. 30 minutes

Ingredients
1 medium pumpkin
3 large onion
3 large potatoes
Oil (soybean oil)
1 can of coconut milk
600 ml vegetable broth
salt and pepper
Nutmeg
Cumin
Curry Powder
½ teaspoon cinnamon powder
Chilli powder

Preparation
Remove the skin and seeds from the
pumpkin and cut into cubes. Peel and dice
the onions and potatoes as well and fry

them together with the pumpkin flesh in soy oil (can also be other oil). Sweat curry powder briefly and deglaze with broth. Bring to the boil once and simmer on a low flame until pumpkin and potatoes are soft. Then add coconut milk and puree. Season to taste with the remaining spices (be very careful with cinnamon), bring to the boil once and pass through a sieve if you like.

RED LENTIL CURRY WITH COCONUT MILK

Menu type: Main course
Servings: 3

Working time approx. 15 minutes
Cooking time approx. 30 minutes
Total time approx. 45 minutes

Ingredients
400 g potato, waxy
200 g lentils, red
1 tablespoon of olive oil
1 bunch spring onion
2 tablespoons curry powder
2 tablespoons tomato paste
400 ml coconut milk
250 ml vegetable broth
salt and pepper

Preparation
Peel, wash and chop the potatoes. Wash the spring

onions and cut into rings, wash the lentils.

Heat the olive oil in a large pot and sauté the spring onions until translucent. Then add the potatoes and fry briefly. Add the tomato paste and curry, then add the lentils.

Now pour the vegetables with coconut milk and vegetable stock and cook for about 25 - 30 minutes. Finally season to taste with the spices.

If the curry gets too thick, simply add more vegetable stock. On the second day it usually tastes even better.

PUMPKIN SOUP WITH RED LENTILS

Menu type: Main course
Servings: 4
Working time approx. 20 minutes

Cooking time approx. 30 minutes

Total time approx. 50 minutes Ingredients
1 large onion
2 chili peppers, depending on pungency and taste
1 piece ginger, peeled, walnut-sized
400 g pumpkin flesh, e.g. from Hokkaido pumpkin
1 bell pepper, orange or red
1 tablespoon pumpkin seed oil
2 tablespoons of olive oil
900 ml vegetable broth
150 ml coconut milk
200 g lentils, red, dried
1 teaspoon lemon peel
salt and pepper

Preparation

Finely dice the onion, the chilies, and the ginger, and coarsely chop the pumpkin and the bell pepper. Put the pumpkin seed and olive oil into a large pot and fry the onions in it at a mild temperature, stirring several times, until they become glassy. Now add chili, ginger, pumpkin and paprika, and also fry briefly. Then deglaze with the vegetable stock and let it cook covered for 10 minutes at medium heat.

Puree the vegetables, then add the coconut milk and the lentils. Cook for another 15 minutes without lid until the lentils are firm to the bite. Stir several times if necessary, the lentils tend to burn. Finally, season with salt, pepper and lemon grated to taste.

CREAM OF MUSHROOM SOUP

Menu type: Main course
Servings: 2

Working time approx. 15 minutes
Cooking time approx. 20 minutes
Total time approx. 35 minutes

Ingredients
150 g mushrooms, fresh
1 small onion
2 tablespoons of butter
Parsley, to taste
2 tablespoons flour
375 ml vegetable stock, hot
125 ml sweet cream
Salt
Pepper, white

Preparation
Wash and slice the mushrooms. Chop

the onion finely. Heat broth.

Melt 1 tablespoon of butter in a small pot
and fry the onion and mushrooms in it.
Add the parsley and set the pot aside.

In another pot, melt the remaining butter,
sprinkle in the flour and fry until light yellow.
Then add the hot broth and bring to the boil
several times while stirring with an egg whisk.
Stir in the cream and season to taste with salt
and pepper, add mushrooms and onions and
stir in well. Add the remaining parsley.

If necessary, refine with a little white wine.

ALPHABET SOUP

Menu type: Main course
Servings: 4

Working time approx. 15 minutes
Cooking time approx. 30 minutes
Total time approx. 45 minutes

Ingredients
100 g pasta (letters)
2 tablespoons heaped vegetable stock, instant
1 liter of water, possibly a little more
1 courgette
2 peppers, red
2 carrot
1 onion
3 tomato, chopped small
possibly herbs, fresh, dried or frozen
salt and pepper
Paprika powder, noble sweet
1 tablespoon of olive oil

Preparation
Chop or chop the onions finely and then sauté
them with the olive oil in a large pot. Then
add the water and while it starts boiling, slice

the peeled carrots directly into the pot.

When the water boils, stir in the broth. Cut the zucchini into cubes or halved slices and then add them to the soup together with the noodles. Simmer for about 20 minutes and then add the chopped tomatoes and peppers.

Add some water if necessary. Simmer for another 10 minutes and season to taste with spices, salt, and pepper.

CABBAGE SOUP

Menu type: Main course
Servings: 4

Working time approx. 20 minutes
Cooking time approx. 45 minutes
Total time approx. 1 hour 5 minutes

Ingredients
1 small white cabbage
300 g minced meat
1 large onion, chopped
3 medium potatoes, quartered
2 medium carrot
1 tablespoon, strudel caraway, whole
some salt
some pepper
1 teaspoon, heaped broth, granulated
1 liter of water

Preparation
Sauté the chopped onion in the pot until transparent and add the chopped onion. Season with salt and pepper. You can add a little more salt and pepper to the mince, it will later be lost in the soup. Peel and quarter the potatoes,

cut the cabbage and carrots into bite-size
pieces and add to the fried mince. Add as much
water (approx. 1-2 liters) until everything is
just covered. Add the caraway and the stock,
if necessary season with salt and pepper
and let it simmer for about 30 minutes.

PUMPKIN CREAM SOUP

Menu type: Main course
Servings: 4

Working time approx. 25 minutes
Cooking time approx. 40 minutes
Total time approx. 1 hour 5 minutes

Ingredients
800 g pumpkin flesh, without skin and seeds
1 medium-sized onion
2 cloves of garlic
750 ml chicken broth (soup)
200 ml cream (cream)
Butter
Pumpkin seed oil
Pumpkin seeds
Salt
Pepper

Preparation
Dice the pumpkin flesh.
Chop onion and garlic finely and fry in some
butter. Add the pumpkin flesh, fry briefly

and then add the soup. Season with salt and pepper. Cover and cook for half an hour, then add 150 ml cream. Bring to the boil again and puree with a hand blender. Season to taste.

Beat the rest of the cream until stiff. Coarsely chop 2 tablespoons pumpkin seeds. Serve the soup.

GYRO SOUP

Menu type: Main course
Servings: 8

Working time approx. 1 hour
Rest period approx. 12 hours
Total time approx. 13 hours

Ingredients
1 kg of meat (gyros meat)
3 cups of whipped cream
375 g onion
75 g butter
1-liter meat stock
4 tablespoons white wine
1 tin of corn
2 red bell peppers
½ Glass of sauce (gypsy sauce)
½ Glass of chili sauce
salt and pepper

Preparation
Brown the fresh gyros meat well, then add the whipped cream. Place everything in a large saucepan and leave to soak overnight in a cool place.

The next day prepares the onion soup in an

extra pot: Peel and slice the onions. Melt the butter and sauté the onion slices in it. Add the meat stock and cook the onions in it until done. Finally, add the white wine.

Cut the peppers into small strips and cook them with the onion soup. Then add the onion soup to the meat-cream mixture in the large pot. Add the corn, gypsy sauce, and chili sauce as well and cook everything at low heat for about 30 - 45 minutes. Attention: The gyro soup must not boil! Finally, season to taste with a little salt and pepper.

PEA SOUP

Menu type: Main course Portions: 3

Working time approx. 30 minutes
Rest period approx. 12 hours
Cooking time approx. 2 hours
Total time approx. 14 hours 30 minutes

Ingredients
150 g peas, dried
½ Litres of water
150 g bacon, in one piece
100 g leek, cut into thin rings
100 g carrot (roots), finely diced
50 g celery, peeled, in one piece
150 g potato, finely diced
1 bay leaf
1 onion, finely diced
1 tablespoon of oil
250 ml meat broth
Pepper
250 g Mettenden preparation soak the
peas in 1/2 l water overnight.

The next day brings to the boil with the water.
After about half an hour add the belly bacon

and cook everything for another half hour. Add the leek rings, carrot and potato cubes, and the bay leaf. Fry the onion cubes in hot oil in a small pan, then add them to the soup as well. Add the piece of celery. Add the meat stock and cook the soup for another half hour.

After this time, remove the celery, bay leaf, and belly bacon.

Now either puree the soup by hand with a masher or briefly hold a blender in. Cut the belly bacon into small pieces and put it back into the soup, together with the ends of the mead. Season to taste with pepper. Salting is usually not necessary because of the bacon and the mead ends.

Finally, let it simmer for another half an hour on the lowest cooking level, stirring every now and then. Serve hot.

PARSNIP CREAM SOUP

Menu type: Main course
Servings: 6

Working time approx. 15 minutes
Cooking time approx. 25 minutes
Total time approx. 40 minutes

Ingredients
500 g parsnip
250 g potato, floury
1 tablespoon butter or margarine
80 ml white wine
1-liter broth
Nutmeg
salt and pepper
375 g cream
1 tablespoon butter
1 tablespoon parsley, chopped

Preparation
Peel the parsnips and potatoes. From one parsnip,
scrape off about 18 thin slices (for decoration).
Cut the rest of the parsnips and potatoes into

small cubes and sauté them in butter or margarine in a pot. Then deglaze with white wine and let it boil down, add broth, season and simmer for about 15 minutes with lid. Meanwhile, melt the butter in a pan and slowly fry the parsnip slices in it until they are crisp and brown. Keep warm afterward. Whip 75 g cream until stiff. Then puree the soup finely with a hand blender, mixing in 300 g of cream and seasoning again. Scoop into plates and serve with a dollop of whipped cream, the fried parsnip slices and the chopped parsley.

GOULASH SOUP

Menu type: Main course
Servings: 4

Working time approx. 40 minutes
Total time approx. 40 minutes

Ingredients
500 g beef from the leg
3 large onion
30 g clarified butter or lard
2 tablespoons tomato paste
salt and pepper, from the mill
1 teaspoon paprika powder, rose hot
1 teaspoon paprika powder, noble sweet
1 pinch of caraway
1 pinch of marjoram
1-liter meat stock
2 peppers, red and yellow
1 can of tomato, peeled
4 large potatoes
1 glass of red wine
Chilli pepper or Tabasco

Preparation
Cut the beef into cubes of about 1 cm.

Peel the onions and also dice them.
Heat the lard in a large pot and gradually fry the meat vigorously on all sides. Add diced onion and tomato paste and fry. Season with salt, pepper, the two types of paprika, marjoram and caraway. Add the meat stock, bring to the boil and simmer covered for 50 minutes. In the meantime, cut the peppers in half, remove the seeds, wash and drain. Cut the peppers into strips and add to the soup. Cook for another 10 minutes, then add the peeled tomatoes to the soup. Peel and dice the potatoes and add them to the soup. Cook for another 20 minutes, then remove the pot from the heat and add the red wine to the soup. Season again and serve the soup very hot.

LENTIL SOUP

Menu type: Main course
Servings: 4

Working time approx. 30 minutes
Total time approx. 30 minutes

Ingredients
25 g butter
2 clove of garlic, crushed or roughly chopped
1 onion, chopped
½ teaspoon turmeric
1 teaspoon spice mixture (Garam Masala)
¼ teaspoon chili powder
1 teaspoon cumin, ground
1 kg tomato, chopped, canned, drained
175 g lentils, red
2 teaspoon lemon juice
600 ml vegetable stock, stock or instant
300 ml of coconut milk
salt and pepper
Coriander green, chopped
Lemon, cut into slices

Preparation
Melt the butter in a pot. Mix the spices in a

small bowl. Sauté the garlic and onion for
2 - 3 minutes while stirring. Add the spices
and steam for another 30 seconds.
Add tomatoes, lentils, lemon juice, vegetable
stock, and coconut milk to the pot and bring
to the boil. Reduce the heat, simmer for 25-30
minutes until the lentils are soft. If the lentils are
too dry, you can add some more water. Season to
taste with salt and pepper and fill into plates. Garnish with coriander and lemon wedges and serve.

PEAS - CURRY - SOUP

Menu type: Main course
Servings: 4

Working time approx. 25 minutes

Ingredients
700 g peas, frozen
1 onion, diced
40 g butter
800 ml vegetable broth
100 g yogurt
200 g sour cream
2 tablespoons curry powder
2 teaspoons flour
Salt
Pepper
Milk
Curry powder

preparation
Fry onions until translucent. Add peas,
sauté briefly. Deglaze with hot broth and
simmer covered for about 10 minutes.

Remove about 1/4 of the peas with a skimmer. Finely mash the remaining peas in the broth. Stir yogurt with sour cream, curry powder, and flour until smooth, add 4 tablespoon Stir the remaining yogurt cream into the soup with a whisk, bring everything to the boil once. Add the retained peas again. Season soup with salt and pepper. Put a spoonful of yogurt cream on each plate, fill up with soup. Season cold milk with salt and pepper and foam up. Pour on the soup and dust with curry powder.

FISH SOUP

Menu type: Main course
Servings: 6

Working time approx. 35 minutes
Cooking time approx. 20 minutes
Total time approx. 55 minutes

Ingredients
1.300 g fish fillet
150 g shrimps
100 g crayfish tails
1 bunch of soup green, crisp
½ Vegetable onion
1 large chili pepper, red, fresh
2 garlic clove
2 tablespoons herb butter or simple butter
some lobster paste and crustacean paste
2 Becher Crème fraîche à 200g
2 glasses of fish stock, 400 ml each
200 ml white wine
2 lemon
Dill
Salt

Preparation

Cut the soup vegetables (2 large carrots, a piece of celery, half a stick of leek - the white one) and the onion into equally large cubes, cut the leek lengthwise in half and cut into strips, chop the garlic and chili pepper.

Sweat everything together in the herb butter. Deglaze with 200 ml white wine and let it boil down a little. Add fish stock with the same amount of water. Stir in the lobster and crust-accan paste and the crème fraîche. Season to taste with salt. Bring everything to the boil briefly.

Now add the fish fillets in not too small pieces, the shrimps and the crayfish tails, and let everything simmer together on a very low heat for 15 minutes.

Lemon quarters and fresh, chopped dill should be served separately, the fish aroma should not be smashed in the pot.

GREEN SPELT SOUP

Menu type: Main course
Servings: 4

Working time approx. 40 minutes
Total time approx. 40 minutes

Ingredients
30 g margarine or butter
1 bunch of soup vegetables
75 g green spelt (green spelt meal) or
5-grain meal, possibly more
1-liter meat stock or vegetable stock
1 egg
1 cup of sour cream
Herbs, chopped

Preparation
Clean the soup green and cut into small cubes
or thin rings. Heat the margarine in a saucepan
and sauté the soup greens. Then add the green
spelt meal and roast briefly. Add the broth and
simmer for 30 minutes. Stir from time to time.

Stir the egg with sour cream until smooth and add. Let the soup thicken and boil up briefly. Stir in chopped herbs to taste.

The soup also tastes very good with 5-grain grist. If you like the soup a bit thicker, you can also use 100 g of coarse meal (that's the way we like it best).

BORSCHT

Menu type: Main course
Servings: 4

Working time approx. 30 minutes
Cooking time approx. 3 hours
Total time approx. 3 hours 30 minutes

Ingredients
400 g soup meat, mixed
1 large carrot
1 large onion
200 g white cabbage
3 Potatoes
2 tablespoons of butter
2 medium-sized tomato
1 bay leaf
4 teaspoon sour cream
1 pinch of pepper, black, freshly ground
1 tablespoon dill, fresh, chopped
1 tablespoon parsley, fresh, chopped
1 large beetroot
⅛ Litre of broth
2 liters of water

Preparation

Wash the meat, dab dry and boil in 2 l water with salt over low heat. Skim off the foam and leave to stand over medium heat for about 2 hours. Remove the meat. Pick up the cooking broth.

Peel and dice the beetroot, carrot and onion. Clean the white cabbage and cut it into thin strips. Heat the butter and fry the vegetables in it. Add about 1/8 liter of stock and stew everything for about 10 minutes at low heat. Add the peeled and sliced potatoes and the bay leaf. Add the rest of the broth through a sieve and cook everything for about 30 minutes.

Scald the tomatoes with hot water, skin and chop them, add dill and parsley to the borscht, and season it with salt and pepper. Now chop the meat into small pieces and add to the soup as well.

COCONUT SOUP

Menu type: Main course
Servings: 4

Working time approx. 15 minutes

Ingredients
½ Litres of coconut milk
½ Litres of chicken stock or vegetable broth, instant
4 Kaffir lime leaves
2 stems lemongrass
2 tablespoons curry paste, green
10 cm galangal or ginger
2 chilies (Thai chili)
500 g chicken breasts
100 g mushrooms (shiitake) or mushrooms
2 tablespoons fish sauce
2 tablespoons cane sugar
4 spring onion
1 handful of coriander
½ Lime, including the juice
possibly vegetables of your choice
possibly basil (Thai basil)

Preparation

Heat the broth together with the coconut milk and curry paste Meanwhile peel and slice the galangal. Wash and halve lemongrass well, beat the thick ends with a meat tenderizer or a pan to bring out the aromas. Cut lime leaves into very fine strips. Add everything to the coconut stock and simmer gently for about 10 minutes.

In the meantime halve the chilies, remove the seeds and cut into fine strips. Cut chicken, mushrooms and vegetables into bite-sized pieces. Fish lemongrass out of the soup and add the Ingredients that you have just cut. Simmer again for 10 - 15 minutes until everything is cooked.

Season with fish sauce, sugar, and the juice of the lime. Arrange the soup and garnish generously with the plucked herbs.

CRAB SOUP

Menu type: Main course
Servings: 4

Working time approx. 30 minutes
Total time approx. 30 minutes

Ingredients
1 medium-sized onion
1 clove garlic
1 tablespoon margarine
1 tablespoon of flour
2 tablespoons tomato paste
1 pack cream cheese (brunch paprika-pepperoni)
500 ml vegetable broth or fish stock
¼ Litres of cream
salt and pepper
200 g prawns
some Tabasco or
Sambal Oelek
Parsley

Preparation
Peel and finely chop onions and garlic. Sauté
in margarine until transparent. Sprinkle with
flour and stock. Add tomato paste and brunch.

Season to taste with salt and pepper and Tabasco, add cream and prawns. Simmer briefly, sprinkle finely chopped parsley over it. Shrimps must not cook for long, they become smaller and firmer. -

COCONUT
- GINGER -
CARROT SOUP

Menu type: Main course
Servings: 4

Total time approx. 45 minutes

Ingredients
1 kg carrot, peeled, cut into thin wheels
1 onion, finely chopped
1 piece of ginger, good thumb size or larger
4 potatoes
1 can of coconut milk
½ Litres of vegetable stock
2 tablespoons lime juice
1 tablespoon honey
salt and pepper
1 bunch coriander green

Preparation
Steam onions in a little oil over medium heat
for 5 minutes. Add carrots and ginger, steam

for another 5 minutes. Then add the vegetable stock and the peeled, diced potatoes and cook until the vegetables are soft (approx. 25 min). Leave to cool. Puree the vegetable soup with the blender. Then add the coconut milk, lime juice, and honey and warm it up only slightly. Season to taste with salt and pepper. Sprinkle with chopped coriander leaves before serving. If the soup is too thick, it can be diluted with vegetable stock.

CURRY SAUSAGE SOUP

Menu type: Main course
Servings: 4

Working time approx. 10 minutes
Cooking time approx. 20 minutes
Total time approx. 30 minutes

Ingredients
5 fried sausages, coarse
1 onion
1 red bell pepper
1 can of tomatoes, chunky
200 ml vegetable broth
3 tablespoons curry powder
20 g margarine
2 tablespoons xylitol (sugar substitute)

Preparation
Cut the onion and the paprika into small cubes. Cut the sausages into slices.
Melt 20 g margarine in a pan. First fry the onion, then the sausages. When the sausages are almost ready, add the peppers.

Prepare 200 ml vegetable stock and
mix 2 tablespoons of xucker in it.
Add the tomatoes to the pan and stir. Add 200
ml vegetable stock and simmer for 5 - 10 min.
Finally, add the curry powder and stir again.

PUMPKIN COCONUT SOUP WITH RED LENTILS

Menu type: Main course
Servings: 4

Working time approx. 15 minutes
Cooking time approx. 20 minutes
Total time approx. 35 minutes

Ingredients
200 g pumpkin, seeded and peeled
250 g lentils, red
250 ml of coconut milk
1 onion
Garlic
½ tablespoon Curry
1 red bell pepper
800 ml vegetable broth
1 bunch spring onion
1 piece of ginger

2 tablespoons of oil
Sea salt
Chilli powder
Sugar

Preparation
Wash and drain the red lentils. Wash,
peel, core, and chop the pumpkin, onions,
garlic, paprika, spring onions, and ginger
as required. Dice pumpkin and paprika
more coarsely than ginger or garlic.

Heat 2 tablespoons of oil in a saucepan, fry
the diced onion in it. Then add the rest of the
diced Ingredients, dust with curry and fry
further. Then add vegetable stock and simmer
for about 10 minutes until the lentils are
soft. Add the coconut milk and heat. Finally
season with salt - and if you like it hotter with
chili. A small pinch of sugar is not a must,
but in my opinion, it rounds off the taste.

In the end, puree the soup to
taste or serve as a stew.

KOHLRABI - POTATO - SOUP

Menu type: Main course Portions: 4

Working time approx. 30 minutes
Total time approx. 30 minutes

Ingredients 2 kohlrabi
1 kg potato
1 stick of leek
100 g bacon (belly bacon), smoked
1 onion
400 g minced meat, half and half
1 ½ Litre of broth, strong
200 ml cream
200 g processed cheese, cream
3 tablespoons of flour
2 tablespoons butter, or margarine
salt and pepper
Nutmeg
Parsley

Preparation
Peel kohlrabi and potatoes, cut into cubes of the
same size. Clean the leek and cut it into strips.

Cook in the broth for approx. 10 minutes until al dente, pour into a sieve, collect the broth.

Finely dice the bacon and onion and fry lightly in the fat. Add the minced meat and also fry (not too dark). Dust the flour over it, stir and deglaze with the stock while stirring vigorously. Add the cream and simmer for 2 minutes. Dissolve the cheese in it and season to taste with the spices. Add the vegetables and sprinkle with parsley as desired.

PAPRIKA SOUP

Menu type: Main course
Servings: 4

Total time approx. 15 minutes

Ingredients
1 kg sweet pepper, mixed
2 large onion, diced
3 garlic clove, finely chopped
1-liter vegetable stock
1 cup of crème fraîche
some olive oil, for frying
salt and pepper
Balsamic vinegar

Preparation
Cut the peeled peppers (red, green, and yellow
in equal parts) into cubes, dice the onions
as well, and fry everything together in olive
oil in a pot for about 5 minutes. Now salt the
vegetables a little bit. Then add the vegetable
stock, add the garlic (if you sauté it, there is a
risk that it will become bitter), and let the soup
simmer for 20-30 minutes with the lid closed.

When everything is cooked soft, stir in the

crème fraîche and finely puree the soup
with a hand blender. Heat again on the stove
and season with salt, pepper, and balsamic
vinegar. The balsamico gives a great taste in
addition to the sweetness of the peppers.

CUCUMBER SOUP

Menu type: Main course
Servings: 6

Working time approx. 10 minutes
cooking time approx. 1 hour
Total time approx. 1 hour 10 minutes

Ingredients
2 ½ Litres of water
3 large potatoes
600 g chicken wings or pork ribs
2 carrot
1 piece of celery
1 parsley root
4 Pickled gherkin, firm
1 tablespoon butter
½ Glass of cucumber liquid
some pimento
4 bay leaves
75 ml cream
1 tablespoon of flour
3 tablespoon of dill, fresh, chopped
1 cube chicken stock
some salt and pepper

Preparation

Grate the cucumbers, collect the juice of the cucumbers, and put aside for the time being. Fry the grated cucumbers briefly in hot butter. Then add the flour and sweat for about 3 minutes, put aside.

Prepare the meat-vegetable broth at this time. To do this, bring the water to the boil in a large pot and then add the meat. Add 1 cube of chicken stock, allspice and bay leave. Cook for about 15 minutes (ribs need longer).

In the meantime, peel and chop the vegetables and potatoes and add them. Cook the vegetables for about 20 minutes with the meat and then add the cucumbers first. Then add the cucumber liquid. Cook for another 10 minutes. While stirring slowly add the cream and add the dill. Season to taste with salt and pepper.

BRUSSELS SPROUT SOUP

Menu type: Main course
Servings: 12

Working time approx. 20 minutes

Ingredients
500 g Brussels sprouts, fresh
400 g potato
300 g carrot, fresh
1 bunch of soup greens (soup vegetables,
root vegetables), fresh
1 large onion
250 g sausages, Viennese
3.000 ml vegetable stock, from instant powder
2 bay leaves
1 teaspoon strained pepper, colorful from the mill
3 tablespoons of oil, tasteless (e.g. safflower oil)
1 bunch of parsley

Preparation
The indicated quantities are approximate
values, it does not matter so exactly.

Washing vegetables, cleaning. Leave sprouts whole, peel potatoes and cut into bite-sized pieces, sliced carrots, diced celery, sliced leek (leek), dice onion, chop parsley. Slice sausages; prepare vegetable stock.

Heat the oil and sauté all the vegetables, except the parsley, in it. Deglaze with hot vegetable stock, add sausages, pepper (no salt!) and simmer for 20 minutes at moderate heat, stirring occasionally. When serving, sprinkle with some chopped parsley.

AJVAR SOUP

Menu type: Main course
Servings: 6 Bread

Working time approx. 20 minutes
Cooking time approx. 30 minutes
Total time approx. 50 minutes

Ingredients
1 kg minced meat
1 onion, diced
750 ml water
3 cubes of vegetable stock
250 ml of chili sauce
½ Glass Ajvar mild (340 ml glass)
½ Glass Ajvar sharp (340 ml glass)
200 g processed cheese with herbs
1 cup of sour cream

Preparation
Fry the minced meat with the onion, add the
water and season with stock cubes, chili sauce,
ajvar, herb melted cheese. Let it boil for about
half an hour. Finally, fold in 1 cup of sour cream.

OXTAIL SOUP

Menu type: Main course
Servings: 4

Working time approx. 30 minutes
Total time approx. 30 minutes

Ingredients
500 g oxtail
2 Onion
3 tablespoons soup green, coarsely chopped
2 tablespoons of grease
1 ½ Litres of water
2 bay leaves
2 tablespoons of grease for baking
3 tablespoons of flour
1 tablespoon paprika powder
1 cup red wine, strong
salt and pepper
Sugar
Peppers

Preparation
Have the butcher cut the oxtail into finger-
long pieces.
Peel the onions cut them into slices and roast

them in a pot in the fat until golden brown, take them out of the pot and fry the oxtail in the remaining fat vigorously. Add the soup vegetables and bay leaves, also fry briefly and add the onions again. Fill up with water, salt lightly and cook the meat until soft, it must come off the bone easily, this takes at least 1 ½ hours. It is quicker with the pressure cooker.

Remove the oxtail pieces and remove the meat from the bones. Strain the broth.

Prepare a rather dark roux from fat, flour, and a pinch of sugar, fill up with the cooking stock while stirring constantly, season with salt, paprika, and pepper and boil thoroughly. Add the meat that has been removed from the bone back into the soup and refine it with red wine.

BEAN STEW

Menu type: Main course
Servings: 4

Working time approx. 15 minutes
Cooking time approx. 20 minutes
Total time approx. 35 minutes

Ingredients
1 tin of kidney beans, approx. 400 g
1 tin of beans, white, approx. 800 g
1 tin of tomato, chunky, approx. 400 g
500 ml vegetable broth
2 peppers, red
1 large onion
2 cloves of garlic
2 tablespoons balsamic vinegar
Olive oil
salt and pepper
Nutmeg
Chilli powder
1 bay leaf

Preparation
Chop the onions, garlic, and peppers into small
pieces. Sauté the onions and garlic in olive oil,

add the peppers and beans and deglaze with the chopped tomatoes and vegetable stock.

Add the balsamic vinegar and the spices as desired and simmer for about 20 minutes at medium heat. Season to taste again before serving.

ZUCCHINI SOUP

Menu type: Main course
Servings: 4

Working time approx. 25 minutes
Cooking time approx. 20 minutes
Total time approx. 45 minutes

Ingredients
1 large zucchini (approx. 600 grams)
2 garlic clove
750 ml vegetable broth
125 ml cream
salt and pepper

Preparation
cut the zucchini unpeeled into small cubes,
chop the garlic finely and bring to the boil with
the stock, now add the meatballs and simmer
for another 15 minutes. puree the soup

Stir in the cream, do not let it boil anymore and
season with salt and pepper. Put the balls back
in and let them simmer for a few more minutes.

FISH SOUP

Menu type: Main course
Servings: 4

Working time approx. 20 minutes

Ingredients
2 Onion
200 g carrot
1 potato
1 celeriac
1-liter fish stock (from heads and bones of fish)
600 g fish, (cod, haddock, halibut, salmon
½ Lemon, the juice
3 eggs, of which the yolk
125 ml sour cream
Salt
Pepper, white
Parsley
1 stick of leek
1 stick of celery
125 ml sweet cream

Preparation
Chop the onion. Cut carrots, carrots, and celery
into small cubes, leek and celery stalk into thin

slices, and cook in the fish stock for about 12 minutes. Sprinkle the prepared washed and boned fish with lemon juice, salt, cut into pieces, and add to the vegetables in the fish stock. Cook for another 12 minutes at low temperature. Whisk the egg yolks with sweet and sour cream and half a cup of fish stock and add to the soup, but do not let it boil. Season to taste with pepper, salt, and sprinkle with chopped parsley.

TOMATO SOUP WITH FETA

Menu type: Main course
Servings: 16

Working time approx. 30 minutes
Cooking time approx. 2 hours
Total time approx. 2 hours 30 minutes

Ingredients
6 kg strained tomatoes
12 Onion
16 garlic clove
10 teaspoons oregano
8 teaspoons thyme
4 teaspoons basil, dried
8 bay leaves
12 Cloves
4 tablespoons honey
8 tablespoons vegetable stock powder, instant
800 g feta cheese
500 g cream
salt and pepper
Olive oil

Preparation

Peel onions and garlic cloves. Then chop them and fry them in hot olive oil over moderate heat. Crush or chop the canned tomatoes and add them. Except for cream and feta cheese, add all other Ingredients as well - don't be afraid of the cloves, the soup doesn't taste like it, but they give it the ultimate kick! Cook for at least 2 hours at low heat, stirring from time to time.

Shortly before eating, add the cream and diced feta cheese and only then season with salt and pepper as required.

VEGETABLE SOUP

Menu type: Main course
Servings: 4

Working time approx. 10 minutes
Cooking time approx. 15 minutes
Total time approx. 25 minutes

Ingredients
1 tablespoon butter
1 bunch of soup vegetables
500 ml water, more if necessary - depending
on the amount of soup green
1 teaspoon, heaped salt
½ teaspoons pepper, black, freshly ground
½ teaspoons garlic powder, or soy sauce

Preparation
Cut the celery into small cubes, slice the
carrots and leek and chop the parsley finely.

Melt the butter in a pot and fry the celery and
carrots until soft. Then add the leeks (they do not
take as long as the other vegetables) until they

are soft. Then add as much water as you like and add the parsley and all the spices. If you are not so fond of garlic, you can also use soy sauce as a seasoning. Simmer everything for about 5 minutes.

CHESTNUT SOUP

Menu type: Main course
Servings: 4

Total time approx. 30 minutes

Ingredients
300 g chestnuts, (peeled and cooked)
1 carrot
1 stick of leek, (thin)
40 g butter
salt and pepper
Nutmeg, freshly grated
125 ml wine, white
500 ml of meat broth
200 g whipped cream
1 pinch of cinnamon
Chives, in small roles as a garnish
Icing sugar

Preparation
Put some chestnuts aside for the garnish, cut
the rest into cubes. Cut the cleaned leek into
fine rings, the cleaned carrot into cubes. Foam
the butter in a pot, add the chestnuts and dust
with icing sugar - let the whole thing caramelize

slightly. Add the vegetables and sauté. Season with salt, pepper, the freshly grated nutmeg and deglaze with the wine. Let it boil down. Pour in broth and cream and cook everything over low heat for about 15 minutes until soft. Then puree the soup with a hand blender and season to taste. Divide the soup between the plates, dust with cinnamon, add the chestnuts that have been set aside (preferably halved or diced, whole they are somewhat large), and sprinkle with the chive rolls. Apply and enjoy it.

OATMEAL SOUP

Menu type: Main course
Servings: 5

Working time approx. 30 minutes
Cooking time approx. 15 minutes
Total time approx. 45 minutes

Ingredients
10 tablespoons oat flakes
1 liter of water
1 cube broth
salt and pepper
some butter
Parsley
1 egg

Preparation
Slowly roast the oat flakes in a pot until they are golden brown and fragrant. If you like, you can also put a little butter in the pot to roast.

When the oat flakes have been roasted, add water and bring to the boil once. Now add the stock cube (if you have fresh stock, you can also use it instead of water and stock cubes).

Now let the mixture simmer at medium temperature until the oat flakes have swollen nicely (about 10 minutes). If you like, you can add some more finely chopped parsley. At the end season with salt, and pepper.

If you like, you can skim some soup and let it cool down. Then whisk in egg in it, take the soup off the stove and stir in quickly. Do not let it boil afterward!

ASPARAGUS SOUP

Menu type: Main course
Servings: 4

Working time approx. 45 minutes
Total time approx. 45 minutes

Ingredients
250 g asparagus, white
500 ml water
1 teaspoon salt
2 teaspoons sugar
30 g butter
250 ml milk
15 g wheat flour
1 egg yolk
2 tablespoons whipped cream

Preparation
Peel the asparagus from top to bottom, making sure that the skins are completely removed but not damaging the heads. Cut off the lower ends (remove the woody parts completely). Wash the asparagus, drain and cut into 3 cm long pieces.

Bring the water with salt, sugar, and some butter to the boil in a large pot. Add the asparagus skins and cuttings, bring to the boil, cover and cook gently for about 20 minutes. Then put them in a sieve and collect the asparagus stock.

Put the asparagus stock back into the pot and bring it to the boil with the milk. Add the asparagus pieces, bring to the boil and cook for 8 - 10 minutes. Put the asparagus pieces into a sieve to drain, collect the asparagus stock, and measure 500 ml of it, if necessary fill up with water.

Melt the remaining butter in a pot. Heat the flour while stirring until it is light yellow. Gradually pour on the asparagus stock and whisk through with a whisk, taking care not to form lumps. Bring the soup to the boil and cook for about 5 minutes. Season to taste with salt and pepper.

Whip the egg yolk with the cream, drain the soup with it (do not let it boil) and add the asparagus pieces to the soup.

CABANOSSI - CHEESE - SOUP

Menu type: Main course
Servings: 4

Working time approx. 30 minutes
Total time approx. 30 minutes

Ingredients
250 g Cabanossi
1 medium-sized onion
500 g potato
400 g carrot
1 leek stick
30 g margarine
1 tablespoon of flour
250 ml vegetable broth
250 g cream
200 g processed cheese with herbs
1 bunch of parsley, chopped
salt and pepper

Preparation
Cut the cabanossi into slices. Clean and wash
the vegetables. Chop the onion finely. Cut

the potatoes into small cubes, the carrots into slices, and the leek into rings.

Now heat the margarine in a pot and fry the cabanossi slices in it. Add the onion cubes and fry gently. Dust with flour. Then pour on the stock while stirring. Bring everything to the boil briefly. Add the cream and stir in. Now add potatoes and carrots and cook everything at medium heat for about 12 minutes. Add the leek rings and the processed cheese. Continue cooking the soup until the cheese is completely melted. Season to taste with salt and pepper and finally serve sprinkled with the chopped parsley.

MUSHROOM SOUP

Menu type: Main course
Servings: 4

Working time approx. 30 minutes
Total time approx. 30 minutes

Ingredients
1 large onion
350 g potato, floury cooking
1 tablespoon butter
1-liter meat stock
150 g porcini mushrooms, small
2 egg yolks
150 g sour cream/sour cream
2 tablespoons dill tips
salt and pepper, white

Preparation
Peel and finely dice the onion. Peel and wash potatoes, cut into small cubes. Heat butter in a pot and fry onions until translucent. Steam the potatoes briefly. Pour on broth, cover, and let simmer at low heat for about 10 minutes.

Clean and clean the mushrooms, cut them into fine slices. Add to the stock, cover, and simmer for about 20 minutes at low heat.

Whisk egg yolks with sour cream. Remove soup from the heat. Stir in egg cream, season with salt and pepper and serve sprinkled with dill tips.

POTATO AND GREEN ASPARAGUS SOUP

Menu type: Main course
Servings: 4

Working time approx. 15 minutes
Cooking time approx. 30 minutes
Total time approx. 45 minutes

Ingredients
4 medium-sized potatoes, peeled
and roughly diced
8 asparagus spears, green, cut
into about 2 cm pieces
1 medium onion, peeled and roughly diced
1-liter vegetable stock, preferably organic
125 g crème fraîche
1 shot of white wine, to deglaze
2 shots of olive oil

Preparation

Heat olive oil in a pot and fry the onions and potatoes at medium temperature for about 2-3 minutes. Deglaze with the broth and bring to the boil and simmer until the potatoes are done.

Then fry the asparagus in a pan with a little olive oil, and when it has taken on some color, add a dash of white wine. Wait until the white wine has boiled over and then add the asparagus to the soup. Let it simmer for about 5 minutes, then try if the asparagus is soft. Remove the soup from the stove and puree it with a hand blender.

Add the crème fraîche and mix again vigorously.

SWEET POTATO AND PEANUT SOUP

Menu type: Main course
Servings: 4

Working time approx. 35 minutes
Cooking time approx. 25 minutes
Total time approx. 1 hour

Ingredients
1 onion
1 garlic clove
some olive oil
3 sweet potato (approx. 500 g or a little more)
1-liter vegetable stock
75 g peanuts without shell and some for topping
1 can of coconut milk (400 g)
2 tablespoons lime juice
salt and pepper

Preparation
This delicious sweet potato soup with peanuts

is made very quickly and easily, just like all other soups. But the best thing about this soup is that it is vegan and no meat or other animal products are missing. Especially in winter, this soup is the perfect pick-me-up.

Peel and chop the garlic and onion. Put some olive oil in a large pot and sauté the garlic and onion. Peel and dice the sweet potatoes as well, then put them into the pot and cover them with vegetable stock. Bring to the boil and simmer for 15 - 20 minutes until the sweet potatoes are soft.

In the meantime, peel the peanuts. When the sweet potatoes are soft, mash the soup. Then stir in the coconut milk and also mix in the peanuts. Season to taste with lime juice, salt, and pepper and sprinkle the remaining peanuts over it before serving.

ROSEMARY SOUP

Menu type: Starter
Servings: 8

Working time approx. 20 minutes

Ingredients
2 shallot
2 tablespoons of butter
8 twig(s) of rosemary
250 g mushrooms, white
600 ml of poultry stock
250 ml cream
salt and pepper, from the mill
Sugar
2 chicken breasts, without skin and bone
Honey
clarified butter

Preparation
Dice the shallots very finely and fry them gently
in the hot butter. Clean and dice the mushrooms,
add them, and fry them. Remove the lower
needles from the rosemary, leaving only a little
green at the top. The stems are then used for the
skewers. Fry the rosemary needles as well.

Add the poultry stock and bring to the boil. Then remove from the heat and leave to stand for an hour with the lid closed. Then drain the vegetables through a sieve (do not squeeze, do not puree!). Add the cream to the soup and bring to the boil again. Season to taste with salt, pepper, and sugar.

Cut the chicken breast fillets into even cubes and put them on the rosemary skewers. Season with salt and pepper and fry in hot clarified butter.

Put a blob of honey on the bottom of each of 8 small glasses and pour the hot soup over it. Place the skewers over the edge of the glass and serve immediately.

ONION SOUP

Menu type: Starter
Servings: 4

Working time approx. 20 minutes
Cooking time approx. 25 minutes
Total time approx. 45 minutes

Ingredients
1 kg vegetable onion
5 tablespoons oil, neutral
2 tablespoons flour
salt and pepper, black, freshly ground
2 teaspoons sugar
1-liter vegetable broth, strong
315 ml white wine, dry
50 g butter
5 slices of baguette(s) or toast
8 tablespoons Gruyère, grated
4 teaspoons paprika powder, noble sweet

Preparation
Peel the onions and cut them into fine rings
- this is the original. However, the soup is
sometimes very difficult to spoon, so it is a
good idea to halve or quarter the onions and

then cut or slice them into fine rings.

Heat the oil in a large pot and fry the onions until they are translucent and the onion juice is well-drained. Dust the onions with the flour, season with sugar, salt, and pepper and mix thoroughly. Gradually add the wine first and then the stock and simmer for 15 minutes with the lid slightly open.

Meanwhile, heat the butter in a pan and fry the slices of bread in it until crisp and brown. Again, if you want to have it easier to eat, you should cut the baguette a little smaller, but in the original, whole slices come on top. Of course, these also swim better.

Pour the onion soup into small bowls, place the baguette slices on the onion soup, sprinkle with cheese and paprika. Bake the soup in the oven or under the grill until golden brown and serve immediately.

CLEAR TOMATO SOUP WITH DUMPLINGS

Menu type: Starter
Servings: 2

Working time approx. 45 minutes
Rest period approx. 12 hours
Total time approx. 12 hours 45 minutes

Ingredients
1 ½ Litre of poultry stock, strong
50 g carrot
50 g leek
50 g celery pale
500 g tomato
450 ml canned tomato (Pelati)
2 Branches of tarragon
3 eggs, of which the protein
30 g butter
4 eggs, of which the yolk
50 g white bread, grated
100 g parsley, smooth

salt and pepper
Nutmeg

Preparation

Cut the carrot, leek, and celery into cubes
and add to the cold chicken stock. Scald, peel,
seed, and dice the tomatoes. Coarsely chop
the peeled tomatoes (do not drain the juice!).
Also, add the tomatoes to the chicken stock.
Add the tarragon twigs. Bring to the boil on
medium heat and simmer quietly for about 1
hour. Remove from heat and let it cool down.
Pass through a sieve and collect the soup.
Beat 3 egg whites lightly and fold into the
cold soup, bring to the boil again and pass
through a sieve lined with a cloth. If you like,
you can season the soup with a shot of gin.

Pluck the parsley from the stalks, blanch for a
minute in boiling water, chop with a blender
and pass through a sieve, collecting the puree
(is rather a juice). Cream the butter with the egg
yolk, add the grated white bread and the parsley
puree, season with pepper, salt, and nutmeg, and
knead all Ingredients well. Put the mixture in
the refrigerator for a few hours. Form dumplings
and let them simmer for about 5 minutes in
lightly salted water, which is not yet boiling.

Place the parsley dumplings in preheated plates
and pour the clear tomato soup over them.

BREAD SOUP

Menu type: Starter
Servings: 4

Working time approx. 25 minutes
Total time approx. 25 minutes

Ingredients
1 ½ Litre of broth
½ teaspoon Marjoram, dried
200 g bread, stale, strong (not wholemeal bread)
2 Onion
1 tablespoon lard
2 tablespoons of butter
½ teaspoon caraway, ground
1 small clove of garlic
1 bunch of chives
Salt
Pepper, freshly ground

Preparation
Cut bread into cubes of approx. 1/2-1 cm, fry
lightly in 1-2 tablespoon. butter - put aside.

Brown the onions cut into rings in the
lard and butter mixture (1 tablespoon
lard, 1 tablespoon butter) over mild heat,

stirring frequently, add the caraway seeds and crushed garlic clove - set aside.

Cut the chives into small rolls.

Bring the meat stock with marjoram to the boil, season with salt and pepper.

Put the bread cubes and onion mixture into the plate and fill up with the boiling hot broth. Serve sprinkled with chives.

CUCUMBER SOUP

Menu type: Starter
Servings: 4

Working time approx. 30 minutes

Ingredients
1 cucumber, slim, dark green
100 g crème fraîche
12 walnuts
1 teaspoon salt
1 bunch of dill
1 garlic
some olive oil
salt and pepper, freshly ground
500 g kefir or yogurt

Preparation
Peel the cucumber, halve lengthwise,
and scrape out the seeds with a teaspoon.
Cut the flesh into small cubes, sprinkle
with the salt in a bowl, and chill.

Drain the excess liquid after a while,
squeeze the cucumber cubes a little.

In a bowl, thoroughly mix the peeled, freshly

squeezed clove of garlic with the salt, stir in kefir or yogurt, and crème fraîche thoroughly. After peeling, crush or chop the walnuts in a mortar. Add half of the chopped dill with the nuts to the soup, beat the olive oil into it - how much you take depends on the taste - and season everything with freshly ground pepper to taste.

Put the soup very cold and then spoon it to bread from deep plates on hot summer days. Sprinkle each plate with the remaining dill.

ZUCCHINI SOUP WITH CHEESE

Menu type: Starter
Servings: 4

Working time approx. 15 minutes
Cooking time approx. 15 minutes
Total time approx. 30 minutes

Ingredients
1 kg courgette
60 ml of olive oil
3 garlic clove
750 ml vegetable broth
60 ml cream or cream substitute (soya cuisine)
50 g cheese (e.g., pecorino, Parmesan,
Grana Padano), freshly grated
salt and pepper

Preparation
Cut the zucchini and garlic into slices
and fry them in a pot with heated oil.
Add the vegetable stock, bring to the
boil and simmer for 10 minutes.

Remove the soup from the stove and puree it. Then add the cream or cream substitute and the grated cheese over low heat while stirring. Season to taste with salt and pepper.

PUMPKIN SOUP

Menu type: Starter Portions: 4
Working time approx. 30 minutes

Ingredients
1 small pumpkin (e.g., butternut squash)
1 stick of leek
1 onion
1 piece of ginger, approx. 2 cm,
peeled, cut into sticks
1 garlic clove
700 ml broth, approx.
1 shot of double cream or cream
salt and pepper
1 tablespoon of olive oil
1 teaspoon butter
1 shot of chili oil or pumpkin or walnut oil

Preparation
Clean the pumpkin and the vegetables
and cut them into pieces. In a saucepan,
lightly fry them in some butter and
olive oil (do not let them burn).

Add the stock and simmer on medium
heat for 20 minutes. Puree finely with a

hand blender, then season to taste with
salt, pepper, and double cream.

CHESTNUT CREAM SOUP

Menu type: Starter
Servings: 4

Working time approx. 15 minutes

Ingredients
200 g chestnut (vacuum packed)
2 shallot
2 tablespoons of olive oil
50 ml Madeira or sherry
500 ml vegetable broth
300 ml cream
salt and pepper

Preparation
Peel and finely dice the shallots. Fry in
olive oil until translucent. Add chestnuts
and fill up with Madeira, stock, and cream.
Let simmer for about 5-10 minutes.
Puree with a magic wand and season
to taste with salt and pepper.

RED ONION SOUP

Menu type: Starter
Servings: 5

Working time approx. 30 minutes

Ingredients
500 g onion, red
4 tablespoons of oil
some salt
50 ml red wine
150 ml apple juice
2 tablespoons tomato paste
some chili powder, or a piece of fresh
chili pepper, finely chopped
1-litre meat stock
¼ Vanilla sliced
some pepper
1 teaspoon marjoram, dried
3 slices of rye bread
100 g crème fraîche
4 tablespoons of cream

Preparation

Skin the onions and cut them into fine rings. Heat 2 tablespoons of oil in a frying pan and sauté the onions with some salt for 10 minutes. Stir again and again. Remove 4 tablespoons of the steamed onions and set aside. Pour red wine over the remaining onions and reduce. Pour on the apple juice and let it boil down as well. Then add the tomato puree, the chili pepper, or chili from the mill and the marjoram and roast briefly. Pour on the stock and season with salt and pepper. Cover and cook for 15 minutes over mild heat.

The slices of bread are diced and gently toasted in the remaining oil in a pan. Move the bread a little to one side and put the onions that were previously put to one side into the pan and fry them as well.

The soup is now seasoned with crème fraîche, cream, salt, and pepper. Now the vanilla pod is removed. Then the soup is pureed.

197

LENTIL STEW

Menu type: Starter
Servings: 4

Working time approx. 30 minutes
cooking time approx. 1 hour
Total time approx. 1 hour 30 minutes

Ingredients
1.500 ml of water
300 g pork belly, smoked
250 g lenses
1 stick of leek
2 medium carrot
possibly celeriac, a small piece
1 bay leaf
1 stem of lovage
120 g spaetzle, dry
1 tablespoon mustard, medium hot
Broth, instant
salt and pepper
Vinegar

Preparation
Bring the water to the boil in a high pot and
boil the belly meat in it for 25 minutes.

Then add the lentils rinsed with water
and cook for another 20 minutes.

In the meantime, clean the leeks, carrots, and
celery and cut into small rings/slices/cubes.
Add the soup vegetables, bay leaf, cabbage (if
you have any) and the spaetzle as well as soup
stock (dosage according to package information
- maybe a little less, since some of the liquid,
has already evaporated). Cook again for about
12-15 minutes. Season to taste with salt, pepper,
vinegar (1-2 tablespoons), and the mustard.

Remove the belly meat, remove the rind,
chop the meat into small pieces, and add
it back to the stew. If necessary, remove
the herb from the stew before serving.

If too much liquid is lost during the cooking pro-
cess or you would like to have more of a thinner
soup, then simply add some more water/broth.
If you like, you can heat up some Wienerle
separately and serve it with the stew.

GREEN SPELT SOUP

Menu type: Starter
Servings: 4

Working time approx. 20 minutes
Cooking time approx. 12 minutes
Total time approx. 32 minutes

Ingredients
1 onion
40 g butter
100 g green spelt, ground
1-liter vegetable stock
125 g cream
Salt
Pepper, freshly ground
Sugar
Nutmeg
1 tablespoon herbs, chopped

Preparation
Peel the onion and chop finely. Melt butter in a pot. Fry the onion cubes until light yellow while stirring. Add the green spelt flour and

steam for a short time while stirring. Pour in the vegetable stock and whisk through everything, taking care not to form lumps. Bring the soup to the boil and cook over low heat without a lid for about 10 minutes, stirring occasionally. Add the cream, heat it up and season the soup with salt, pepper, sugar, and nutmeg. Stir in herbs before serving.

IMPRINT

The German Kitchen
Theaterstraße 8
37073 Göttingen

and

Mindful Publishing
by
TTENTION Inc.
Wilmington - DE19806
Trolley Square 20c

Instagram: mindful_publishing
Contact: mindful.publishing@web.de

Made in the USA
Coppell, TX
27 November 2024

41139193R10111